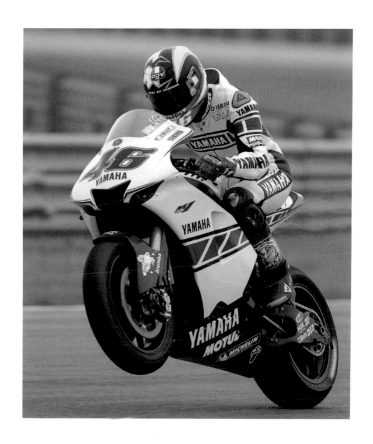

MOTORCYCLE
EVOLUTION • DESIGN • PASSION

MICK WALKER

MOTORCYCLE

EVOLUTION • DESIGN • PASSION

To Gary. A much-missed son and friend

MOTORCYCLE

MICK WALKER

First published in Great Britain in 2006 by Mitchell Beazley,
an imprint of Octopus Publishing Group Ltd

This edition published in 2014 by Bounty Books
a division of Octopus Publishing Group Ltd
Endeavour House,
189 Shaftesbury Avenue,
London WC2H 8JY

www.octopusbooks.co.uk

An Hachette UK Company
www.hachette.co.uk

A CIP catalogue record for this book is available from the British Library.

ISBN: 978-0-753727-63-8

Commissioning Editor **Hannah Barnes-Murphy**
Executive Art Editor **Christine Keilty**
Senior Editor **Suzanne Arnold**
Art Editor/Designer **Colin Goody**
Editor **Ian Penberthy**
Proofreader **Andrew Puddifoot**
Picture Research **Nick Wheldon**
Indexer **Alan Thatcher**
Production **Gary Hayes**

Printed and bound in China

CONTENTS

Foreword 6

Introduction 8

FOREWORD

I was delighted when Mick Walker invited me to write the foreword for his latest book, *Motorcycle*. It is a comprehensive volume that covers all the notable motorcycles and their designers, from Gottlieb Daimler's crude "bone-shaker" of 1885 up to the sophisticated, high-performance machines of today.

Having been a retailer and agent, racer and builder/developer of specialized racing motorcycles myself, I found it fascinating to read how the skills and ideas of the early designers – such as Alfred Angus Scott, the Collier brothers, Edoardo Bianchi, James Lansdowne Norton, Adalberto Garelli, Carlo Guzzi, Edward Turner, Rex McCandless, and many

others – have been built upon by later generations in their constant quest for improvement.

I must admit to being truly amazed, when studying this book, by the sheer breadth and diversity of the subject. While the motorcycles and their designers are central, of course, many giant steps in technical innovation and development have been taken in little over 120 years since Daimler's first two-wheeled prototype appeared.

The early designers were real "artists in metal". Although CAD (computer-aided design) has become a vital tool in the modern motorcycle industry, their ideas, like mine, began with pen and paper or chalk on the floor, followed by hours in the machine shop.

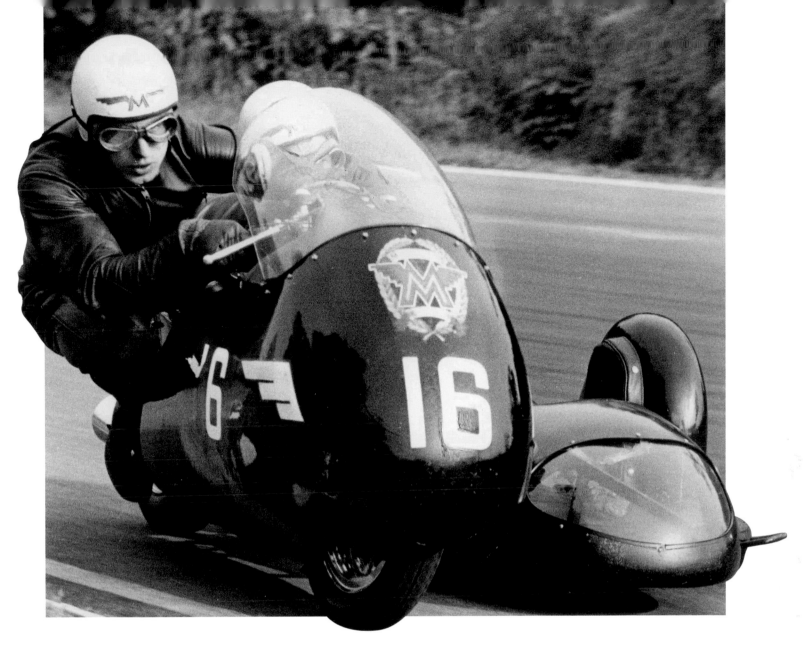

The developments and designs of all the great marques are here, from AJS to Zündapp.

There have been plenty of technical innovations that have played important roles in shaping motorcycle design over the decades. This book examines the most outstanding, such as multi-speed, foot-change gearboxes, methods of lubrication, liquid cooling, final drive, rotary engines, multi-cylinder engines, and turbocharging.

Nowadays, the motorcycle has moved on from its original role of economical personal transport, occupying instead a sophisticated niche in the market of leisure with style. Mick has reflected this shift in the final chapter, "Lifestyle and Leisure", in which he examines custom bikes and retro machines, as well as recent Ducati, Harley-Davidson, and Triumph models, the Yamaha R1, the MV Agusta F4, off-road sport, and the phenomenon of colour coding.

Motorcycle is a thorough and comprehensive book, and it's my pleasure to recommend it.

Colin Seeley

INTRODUCTION

The history of motorcycle design is a fascinating subject, concerning not only the machines themselves, but also the men who created them. Although the motorcycle is as old as its four-wheeled counterpart, far less has been written about its design and development, from the crude motorized two-wheelers of the late 19th century to the 290km/h (180mph) projectiles of the early 21st century. Within the pages of *Motorcycle*, I have attempted to provide a complete insight to this riveting story.

While the German engineer Gottlieb Daimler is credited with producing the first motorcycle powered by an internal-combustion engine, in 1885, there were others who had carried out important work prior to that historic event.

Bicycles came before petrol engines, and steam engines came before both. In fact, the first powered two-wheeler was a cycle equipped with a small steam engine.

The first attempts to provide a two-wheeler with motive power that relied on something other than cranks and pedals occurred during the late 1860s, being inspired by the development of steam power. Steam engines, as epitomized by contemporary rail and road locomotives, were truly massive creations, however, with huge cast-iron cylinders, vast flywheels and heavy connecting rods. Even so, both

Frenchman Pierre Michaux and American Sylvester Howard Roper created steam-driven, two-wheeled machines in 1869. Michaux's device featured a single brazed-steel cylinder, a light steel piston and twin flywheels. Steam was generated by a transverse, multi-tube, cylindrical boiler, heated by alcohol fuel through a series of burners. Roper's machine had a charcoal-fired, twin-cylinder engine. In truth, however, steam power was much more suited to four wheels, because the machinery and boiler could be installed more easily.

During those early pioneering days, inventors experimented with a range of possible power sources for two-wheeled machines. These included compressed air, clockwork, carbonic-acid gas and even hydrogen gas.

The basic principle of the internal-combustion (petrol) engine was outlined by Frenchman Alphonse Beau de Rochas in 1862. Its working application was not patented until 1876, however, by two Germans, Nicolaus Otto and Eugen Langen. The Otto four-stroke cycle of induction, compression, firing, and exhaust remains unchanged today.

Another early pioneer of the motorcycle was Englishman Edward Butler, who employed a two-stroke engine to power a three-wheel machine. This vehicle was patented provisionally in 1884, but it was not actually completed for another four years.

1 THE PION

EERS

THE PIONEERS

The earliest motorcycles were steam driven, but Gottlieb Daimler and his associate, Wilhelm Maybach, produced the first two-wheeler to be powered by an internal-combustion engine. The latter was the work of another pair of Germans, Nicolaus Otto and Eugen Langen.

The fuel Daimler used was known as benzine, but today it is called petrol, one of several distillates of petroleum, or "rock oil" (*petra*, rock; and *oleum*, oil). It is believed that the existence of petroleum and its by-products has been known for over 4,000 years, but only within the past 120 years has it served as one of mankind's most valuable commodities, providing us with unparalleled personal mobility.

One of the world's biggest priorities today is to find a suitable replacement for petrol, because it is a finite resource, but that's another story.

Daimler's creation was largely experimental, acting only as an intermediate stage in his attempt to produce what he called the "four-wheeled, passenger-carrying horseless carriage". It was left to others to further the development of the motorcycle as a form of transport in its own right.

Many pioneering designs were little more than a conventional pedal cycle with an engine attached to the frame. Although a substantial number of the original ideas that caused the birth of the motorcycle came from Germany –

together with the first series-production machines (from the
Munich-based Hildebrand & Wolfmüller factory) – the next
stage of development came from the French and Belgians.

Of particular note were the Russian-born Werner brothers in France, who did much to develop the working utility
motorcycle, popularized the diamond frame, with its central
engine position, dominated many early racing activities and
constructed the first truly practical vertical twin. The
younger Werner, Michel, died at the early age of 46, and
subsequently his brother Eugene's interest waned. When he,
too, died in 1908, the entire Werner enterprise foundered.

Englishman Edward Butler pioneered the use of the two-
stroke engine, employing the pump-type arrangement
patented by Donald Clark in 1880. In this, the injection of a
fresh charge of fuel mixture coincided with the discharge of
burnt gases on the down-stroke of the piston. On the up-
stroke, the gases were compressed, then ignited by an
electric spark to begin the next down-stroke. Butler's Velo-
cycle (three-wheeler) was exhibited as a drawing in 1884
and was not actually built until mid-1888. Thus, it was
preceded by the Daimler Einspur (one track).

GOTTLIEB DAIMLER

Today, the German engineer Gottlieb Daimler (1834–1900) is widely recognized as the "father" of the internal-combustion engine. During the latter half of the 19th century, he collaborated with Wilhelm Maybach to produce the first powered two-wheeler equipped with an internal-combustion engine.

A CRUDE DEVICE

Constructed in 1885, Daimler's machine was a crude device. It had been built as a mobile test rig for the engineer's 264 cc, single-cylinder, four-stroke powerplant. Powered by the new miracle fuel benzine (petrol), this engine had two flywheels, one on each side of the crankshaft, the whole assembly being enclosed within a cast-aluminium crankcase. "Mushroom" valves were used, the inlet being automatically operated by suction of the piston, sitting directly above the cam-operated exhaust valve in a layout known as IOE (inlet over exhaust).

The vehicle was equipped with wooden wheels and a wooden frame, an auxiliary wheel being fitted on each side. It did employ some features, however, that appeared on later motorcycle designs. The rear wheel was belt-driven, for example, while the fan-cooled engine was mounted in the frame on rubber blocks. The engine was started with a crank handle.

With a weight of 90 kg (198 lb), the Daimler machine produced 0.5 bhp at 750 rpm, while the two gear ratios provided speeds of 5 and 11 km/h (3.5 and 7 mph). Other notable aspects of the design included heated tube ignition, an evaporating carburettor and almost conventional handlebars.

THE FIRST TEST RUN

Daimler took out a patent on his design on 29 August 1885, following successful (but very short) test runs in the garden of his house and the streets of Canstatt, South West Germany; the longest journey was some 3 km (1.86 miles). He soon realized, however, that the prototype engine was not really powerful enough and his Petroleum Reitwagen, as he called it, was not easy to ride. It was not only difficult to balance, but also a real "bone-shaker", not helped by the truly dire state of the roads at the time. Consequently, Daimler concentrated his efforts on the development of what would be termed the "horseless carriage" (forerunner of the modern car), having installed one of his later engines in a coach in 1886.

Daimler's original 1885 machine can still be seen in the Daimler-Benz museum in Stuttgart-Untertufürkheim, Germany.

It should be explained that Gottlieb Daimler was a true visionary, who dreamed of his engines serving the whole of mankind. In fact, he lived to see them at work on land, water and air. Although he died three years before the Wright brothers' first powered flight at Kitty Hawk, in the USA, he did witness his engines power a balloon flight and an early motorboat, as well as a wheeled vehicle.

facing page Gottlieb Daimler. In 1885, with associate Wilhelm Maybach, he produced the first two-wheeler with an internal-combustion engine.

above By today's standards, the 1885 Daimler was very crude, having a wooden frame and steel-rimmed wooden wheels.

right The Daimler was powered by a 264 cc, single-cylinder, four-stroke engine.

ALFRED ANGUS SCOTT

Alfred Angus Scott was a visionary designer and a pioneer of the two-stroke motorcycle. His first machine, a 450cc twin, was built in 1908, the concept acting as the basis of some nine decades of two-stroke engine development. This culminated in the near domination of the small-capacity classes by this type of engine, until it was virtually killed off by legislation.

A NATURAL ENGINEERING GENIUS

Alfred Scott cultivated an engine technology that many others would pursue. His basic ideas on the two-stroke cycle endured, albeit modified as technology improved, notably from the early 1960s, when the application of acoustic theory improved gas flow, and materials were developed to withstand the increases in power that this new science provided.

Scott was a natural engineer, who originally designed his creation as a gas engine for boats, his early experiments being carried out on the River Clyde during 1900, and later in cycle frames. The Scott practice of employing a central flywheel, overhung cranks, deflector pistons, and detachable transfer ports started with these early experiments; one motor was constructed with a grooved flywheel that drove the front wheel of a conventional pedal cycle.

The specification of the 450 twin was way ahead of anything else available at the time. In the days of belt drive and bump (push) starting, the Scott excelled in having a chain drive and kickstarter, and was further enhanced by a two-speed gearbox with a central neutral position. Offering a superior performance to the rival single-cylinder four-strokes of the era, the Scott was looked on favourably by the sporting fraternity, much to the distain of other British manufacturers – who

facing page Vintage racer Chris Williams was almost unbeatable for many years with this liquid-cooled Scott. He is shown here winning at Cadwell Park in the summer of 1969.

above right Designed by Bill Cull, Scott's three-cylinder model of the 1930s had the potential to be a superbike of its era. The liquid-cooled engine featured a 120-degree crankshaft, car-type clutch and four-speed gearbox. In all, however, only eight examples were built.

right Far more typical of Alfred Angus Scott's view of two-stroke design is this Flying Squirrel, circa 1930. It has inclined, parallel twin cylinders and a radiator for the liquid cooling system above the engine.

complained bitterly to the sport's controlling body, the Auto Cycle Union. Their main objection was that, whereas their engines fired on every other revolution, the Scott fired on every revolution, which was deemed to be an unfair advantage.

AIR AND WATER COOLING

The original Scott prototype motorcycle and the early production models (1909) featured air-cooled cylinders with water-cooled heads, but soon liquid cooling was utilized for both components.

This unusual cooling arrangement was not the only pioneering feature of Scott motorcycles. In addition to the two-speed gearbox already mentioned, both the rear wheel and primary drives were by chain – at a time when belts dominated. Moreover, the fully triangulated frame was fitted

with a new design of girder front fork with a central spring, which was the forerunner of the later telescopic fork.

The roadster and racing variants of the Scott were distinguished by the colour of their cylinders – red and green respectively.

In the Isle of Man Tourist Trophy (TT) races, the Scott works racers, fitted with rotary inlet and transfer valves, broke the lap record. Wins were recorded in the 1912 and 1913 TTs, while a further lap record was gained in 1914.

The avant-garde nature of Scott's two-strokes did not totally disappear after his death in 1923. Instead, W. (Bill) Cull continued technical development, the results of which included 498- and 596 cc models named the Squirrel. The larger of the two machines was capable of 137 km/h (85 mph) in series-production road trim.

2 BIKES FO

R WAR

above The German BMW company pioneered the use of hydraulically damped telescopic front forks, as fitted to this 1935 R12 750.

left The military began using motorcycles in World War I (1914–18). These machines are Royal Enfield V-twins.

facing page An Indian Chief 1200cc, side-valve V-twin on patrol near the front, circa 1942. This machine was typical of the large-capacity American motorcycles used by Allied forces during World War II.

BIKES FOR WAR

In the military, the motorcycle replaced the horse as an efficient means of carrying despatches, while in sidecar guise, it proved a functional and highly mobile light assault vehicle and transport.

It was during World War I (1914–18) that the motorcycle first displayed its suitability as a war machine, the British forces with their Douglas 350s, Triumph 550s, Rudge Multis, P & Ms, and Royal Enfields leading the way. Following America's entry into the conflict, a host of Excelsiors, Harley-Davidsons, and Indians were shipped across the Atlantic. Other early military motorcycles came from FN (Belgium), NSU (Germany), and Puch (Austro-Hungary).

When Germany invaded Poland on 1 September 1939,

at the start of World War II, many countries in Europe had been gearing up for war for several months, following the Munich Crisis of the previous year. The British Norton company, for example, had foregone its usual challenge for road racing honours during the 1939 season, concentrating instead on military contracts, thanks to the persistence of its managing director, Gilbert Smith.

The machine Norton was building was the 490cc, side-valve, single-cylinder Model 16H. Basically, this was a 1937 civilian model, the military conversion consisting of little more than a crankcase shield, a pillion seat or rear carrier rack, a pair of canvas pannier bags, provision for masked lighting, and an overall coat of khaki paint. Norton's factory in Birmingham also built the very similar Big Four with a larger 634cc engine. Around 100,000 16Hs were built for wartime service, demonstrating how Smith's foresight had paid commercial dividends.

Like the Nortons, many other military motorcycles were little more than revamped civilian models. In modern warfare, however, as in other areas, the development of the motorcycle was unrelenting, and soon more specialized designs began to appear.

Each country's armed forces found they had particular requirements: the British concentrated on simple singles; the Germans favoured complex, horizontally opposed twins; the Americans opted for heavyweight V-twins. The Italians produced some interesting designs, many of them built by companies that were more familiar with grand prix racing than military needs.

In many ways, the motorcycle was the unsung hero of World War II. It carried out a truly amazing variety of tasks, but was used most widely by the famous DRs (despatch riders). Although radio communications had replaced the miles of telephone wire that had been laid near the front lines during World War I, the motorcycle played a vital role in carrying messages and documents.

Other important duties included marshalling road convoys, scouting, and, when coupled to a sidecar, acting as a machine-gun carrier.

AMERICA FLIES THE FLAG

Although America did not officially enter World War II until the Japanese attack at Pearl Harbour in December 1941, within days of Britain and France declaring war on Germany, in September 1939, both governments had placed substantial orders with the American motorcycle industry.

During the conflict, two companies supplied the bulk of the American motorcycle output for European armies, and later for the American and Canadian forces. These were Harley-Davidson and Indian.

To European eyes, the American machines were massive (and heavy!). Most were V-twins with foot-operated clutches and hand-change gearboxes.

HARLEY-DAVIDSON WLA

Essentially, the Harley-Davidson WLA was the civilian 745cc (69.8x96.8mm bore and stroke), side-valve V-twin with a number of modifications to make it suitable for military service. These included a heavy-duty luggage carrier, a rifle scabbard, "blackout" lights at front and rear, and a shield to protect the underside of the engine's crankcase. The military specification also included leather pannier bags, front and rear crash bars, a handlebar-mounted screen, and, of course, an overall coat of drab paint. Other features were a comprehensive air filtration system, footboards, and, quite often, ammunition boxes, which were mounted on the front forks.

The engine was of the traditional Harley-Davidson narrow–angle V-type. If anything, this was over-engineered, the iron cylinders and light-alloy heads being provided with more than adequate finning to ensure sufficient cooling, even during long periods of low-speed running in bottom gear, when acting as convoy escort, for example.

The valves were on the offside (right) of the power unit, the two exhaust header pipes being joined low down to run rearward into a single silencer. Other details included a single Linkert carburettor, coil ignition, a three-speed gearbox, and dry-sump lubrication.

The WLC (Canadian) version featured a hand-operated clutch instead of a foot clutch and hand gearchange. Around 20,000 WLCs were produced, compared with 68,000 WLAs. In Harley "speak", the WL was known as the Flathead 45.

INDIAN 841

Although there were several conventional Indian V-twins (very much in the mould of the Harley-Davidson WLA), an interesting alternative was the Model 841, which had been conceived specifically as a military motorcycle. This was a 745cc (73.0 x 88.9 mm bore and stroke), side-valve, transverse V-twin. Compared with other American designs of the period, it was an advanced machine. As well as state-of-the-art suspension (telescopic front fork/plunger rear), the 841 featured a four-speed, foot-change gearbox instead of the hand-change type favoured by Harley-Davidson. It also had shaft final drive. Although transverse V-twins were nothing new, like the later Moto Guzzi V7 series, the Indian offered excellent cooling, a low centre of gravity, and good performance, with a top speed of 113km/h (70mph).

facing page An American military training college during 1917, with instructor, pupils, and Harley-Davidson V-twin engine.

above During World War II, Harley-Davidson built almost 90,000 WLA (American) and WLC (Canadian) 750cc V-twins for military use.

right Harley-Davidson, inlet-over-exhaust V-twin engine, circa 1917.

BRITISH BULLDOGS

The Allies were victorious in World War II, but which nation's bikes were the most successful in wartime conditions? If quantity is the yardstick, then Great Britain has to be awarded the accolade – British manufacturers produced more military motorcycles during the war than those of any other nation, the most popular types being BSA (126,000, mainly side-valve M20s), Norton (100,000, side-valve 16Hs), AMC (80,000, mostly Matchless G3/Ls), Ariel (47,600, overhead-valve W-NGs), and Royal Enfield (29,000, two-stroke WLs). If the machines supplied by Triumph, Velocette, Cotton, Douglas, James, and Excelsior are included, the total output reaches 420,000 – a staggering figure.

MATCHLESS G3/L
Of all the British four-stroke models, the best all-round machine was the Matchless G3/L. Like the German DKW

RT125, it was a classic design and, in civilian guise, it remained in production until the mid-1960s.

Unlike the German lightweight, however, the Matchless was based on an existing model, the G3. Both had a capacity of 348cc (69.0x93.0mm bore and stroke) and a four-speed, Burman-made, foot-change gearbox.

What really set the G3/L apart from its earlier civilian counterpart was its weight – the military model had been pruned significantly and was 25kg (56lb) lighter.

Most significant of all – at least, as far as British bikes were concerned – was the incorporation of the patented Teledraulic front fork, a design that relied heavily on pre-war BMW technology. This was not only technically superior to the girder types found on other British machinery of the period, but it also improved the bike's aesthetic appearance, giving the newcomer a very modern look.

facing page British motorcycles played a key role in both world wars. This Royal Enfield V-twin sidecar outfit is shown outside the company's Redditch factory in 1917, the sidecar being used as a machine-gun platform.

left British military motorcycle output during World War II reached some 420,000 bikes. Here, production of the 400,000th example is celebrated toward the end of the conflict.

above British parachute troops in 1944 with examples of the Royal Enfield Flying Flea. The machine was one of three designed specifically for airborne use.

The air-cooled, overhead-valve single, with a vertical cylinder, alloy head, coil valve springs, gear-driven cams, and roller-bearing big-end, produced 16bhp and could reach a top speed of 114km/h (71mph).

The machine's only real drawback – when compared with the more bulky (and much heavier) Norton and BSA side-valve singles – was that, because of its sheer compactness, gaining access to some components was difficult and time consuming. Around 60,000 G3/Ls were built for military service.

AIRBORNE BIKES

British airborne forces employed lightweight motorcycles that could be dropped by parachute where needed and quickly assembled in the field. Although others were built in Italy, Germany, and America (all in small numbers), the British had

by far the greatest success with the concept. Specialized machines were built by James, Royal Enfield and Excelsior, all being two-strokes.

Royal Enfield's effort (known as the Flying Flea) was a 126cc (54.0x55.0mm bore and stroke), DKW-based, ultra-lightweight model designed by Ted Pardoe. The James was powered by a 122cc (50.0x62.0mm bore and stroke), Villiers 9D engine with three-speed, hand-change gearbox, and was known as the ML (Military Lightweight).

The most unusual of the trio, however, was Excelsior's folding design, known as the Welbike. This had been designed by Lieutenant-Colonel J.R.V. Dolphin, and was equipped with tiny wire wheels and a 98cc, single-speed, push-start Villiers engine. The machine could be stowed in a standard cylindrical parachute container. After the war, it was fitted with an Excelsior engine and sold as the Corgi.

DKW RT125

Although Alfred Scott was the original pioneer of the two-stroke engine, German companies – first DKW and later MZ – were largely responsible for its evolution.

JÖRGE SKAFTE RASMUSSEN

The founding father of DKW was Jörge Skafte Rasmussen. Born in Denmark in July 1898, he moved with his family to Dusseldorf, Germany, in 1904, then in 1907 to Zschopau, south of Chemnitz in Saxony. Later, he held a number of engineering posts and, after World War I, formed J.S. Rasmussen, the forerunner of DKW.

In 1916, inspired by acute wartime fuel shortages, Rasmussen had begun to experiment with a steam car, the Dampf Kraft Wagen. Although the machine was not put into production, it provided the now-famous DKW initials.

Three years later, in 1919, Rasmussen produced an 18 cc, toy two-stroke engine, together with a 122cc auxiliary engine, both designed by Hugo Ruppe.

WORLD'S LARGEST MOTORCYCLE MANUFACTURER

Rasmussen progressed to building motorized bicycles, "armchair" motorcycles (forerunners of the modern scooter), and, finally, conventional motorcycles. By 1926, DKW had manufactured 100,000 engines (all of them two-strokes), while the motorcycle range included bikes with displacements of 200, 250, 350, and 500cc.

By the time DKW became part of Auto Union, in 1932, it could justifiably claim to be the largest motorcycle manufacturer in the world.

RACING IMPROVES THE BREED

DKW had begun racing two-stroke motorcycles in 1925, the machines having intercooling and the Bichrome system of supercharging. In 1931, chief designer Hermann Weber, assisted by August Prussing, created a split-single design, and from then on until the outbreak of war in 1939, DKW was a dominant force in not only grand prix racing, but also record-breaking in the lightweight (250cc) class.

THE RT125

The company had the largest research and development department in the industry, and all of the technical expertise and experimentation had a knock-on effect on production models. The prime example of this was DKW's most famous and influential bike, the RT125. Designed by Weber, this tiny motorcycle was powered by an all-new, 122cc (52.0x58.0 mm bore and stroke), unit-construction engine with a light-alloy cylinder head and cast-iron barrel.

Despite the rationalization of the German motorcycle industry, carried out in 1938, the RT125 was such an excellent design that it was ordered into production as soon as its test programme had been completed. Its light weight and durability led to its wide use by the German armed forces throughout World War II, particularly for scouting and communications work.

After the end of the war, the RT125 went on to become the most copied motorcycle in history. The British BSA Bantam, American Harley-Davidson two-stroke and Soviet Moska all stemmed from Weber's design.

left Powered by an all-new, 122 cc, piston-port-induction, two-stroke engine with integral three-speed gearbox, the DKW RT125 was the work of the brilliant designer Hermann Weber.

facing page:
top In October 1937, DKW took part in a successful series of record-breaking attempts. Both solo and "sidecar" (shown) versions were used.

bottom Ewald Kluge and Siegfried Wünsche rebuilding a DKW 250cc racing engine. The German government was very keen to support motorcycle sport in the years leading up to World War II.

DKW RT125 SPECIFICATIONS

Engine Air-cooled, piston-port, two-stroke, single-cylinder

Displacement 122cc

Bore and stroke 52.0 x 58.0 mm

Ignition Flywheel magneto

Gearbox Three-speed, foot-change

Final drive Chain

Frame All-steel, welded

Dry weight 68 kg (150 lb)

Maximum power 4.8bhp at 5,000rpm

Top speed 76 km/h (47mph)

3 THE 192

S & 1930S

above left Designed by Val Page, the 647 cc Triumph 6/1 vertical twin preceded Edward Turner's famous Speed Twin by several years. It was introduced in July 1933.

left Folke Mannerstedt returned home to Sweden to join Husqvarna from the Belgian FN company in 1928. One of his first tasks was to build this new 500cc racer powered by a British JAP engine.

above The British Excelsior company won the 1933 Lightweight (250cc) TT with its innovative Mechanical Marvel. The bike featured four radial valves, two carburettors, and a sophisticated dry-sump lubrication system.

facing page A typical British motorcycle of the era, a 1930 twin-port Ariel Model G with 499 cc, overhead-valve engine, hand-change gearbox, rigid frame, girder front fork, and drum brakes.

THE 1920S & 1930S

After World War I (1914–18), the population of Europe had a much better understanding of the mechanical world. At the beginning of the conflict, cavalry had gone to war on horseback; by the end, horses had been replaced by motorized armoured tanks. In virtually every other military arm, the development of machinery had taken place at breathtaking speed.

Throughout Europe, large numbers of new companies were formed to cater for peacetime motorcycling. Some survived for only a few months, whereas others joined the existing motorcycle industry to become major players.

Although motorcycles were manufactured in Czechoslovakia, France, Belgium, Sweden, and Switzerland, the major producers resided in Germany, Italy, Britain, and the United States of America.

Many of the war's largest armaments concerns attempted to grab a slice of the action, but their efforts were often hampered by the damage their factories had received during the conflict. Probably the nearest to success was the British Sopwith company's involvement with the ABC 400cc flat-twin. Although this was an advanced design, with such features as overhead valves and a four-speed gearbox, it suffered from insufficient development, and both ABC and Sopwith went bust during the 1920s.

Much more successful was the German aero engine giant BMW. At first, it only produced engines for other motorcycle firms, but in 1923, the first machine to bear the famous blue and white emblem on its tank appeared at the Paris motorcycle show.

The first truly golden age of motorcycle sales was the 1920s. Then came New York's Wall Street Crash in October 1929. Although America bore the early brunt of this, it was not long before the "Great Depression", as it was called, spread across the Atlantic to Europe, millions being thrown out of work in all the industrialized countries.

The effects of the Great Depression lasted until the mid-1930s, forcing many firms out of business, while others only escaped by the skin of their teeth.

There were several important advances in motorcycle design during the 1920s and 1930s, many the work of notable engineers. Among these were Edward Turner, Valentine Page, Percy Goodman, Arthur Carroll, Walter Moore, George Patchett, James L. Norton, and Harold Willis (Britain); Mario Mazzetti, Alfonso Morini, Adalberto Garelli, Carlo Guzzi, Mario Baldi, Piero Remor, and Carlo Gianni (Italy); Max Fitz, Richard Küchen, Hermann Reeb, Hugo Ruppe, August Prussing, and Hermann Weber (Germany); and Charles B. Franklin and Bill Harley (USA).

After World War II (1939–45), several important manufacturers did not re-open their factories, notably Brough Superior, Böhmerland, Coventry Eagle, Della Ferrera, New Imperial, OK Supreme, and Rudge.

THE SWEDISH INDUSTRY

Although there have been many Swedish motorcycle marques over the years (including Nordstjernan, Nymans, and Monark), one company has dominated – Husqvarna.

The Husqvarna company was formed as early as 1699, when Erik Dahlberg, a leading industrialist and governor of the region in which the town of Huskvarna (note the "k" in place of the "q") was situated, decided to supply much-needed weapons to the Swedish Army. Thus, like BSA in Britain, Husqvarna built its original business upon the arms trade.

With its expertise in precision engineering, Husqvarna was quick to seize the opportunity when the motor age arrived, and in 1903 it began building motorcycles. Its first machines were fitted with imported engines from Moto Rêve, NSU, and FN.

A COMPLETE MOTORCYCLE

The next major step came in 1918, when Husqvarna designed and built its own complete machines for the first time. A large contract from the Swedish Army followed, and the motorcycle side of the business became an important money spinner. It

was then that the company made its first moves into motorcycle sport.

Realizing that competition wins were the finest form of publicity, Husqvarna developed special bikes for long-distance cross-country events, then popular throughout Scandinavia. These, in turn, led to entries in the International Six Days Trial.

The young Swedish engineer Folke Mannerstedt joined the company, having returned from Belgium, where he had worked for FN. One of his first tasks was to design a new racer, which was powered by a British JAP 500 cc, overhead-valve, single-cylinder engine. After indifferent results, however, Mannerstedt, assisted by Calle Heimdahl, set out to build a new engine.

THE V-TWIN

Mannerstedt's first prototype appeared at the 1930 Swedish Grand Prix, and from 1932, it became a serious challenger. The engine was a 497 cc (65.0 x 75.0 mm bore and stroke), 50-degree V-twin with pushrod-operated valves. It produced 44 bhp at 6,800 rpm and was good for 193 km/h (120 mph).

By 1934, it had been improved still further, with larger valves and a stiffened crankcase, resulting in 46 bhp. There was also a 350cc version.

The engine was fairly conventional in that the crankcase was separated vertically, with pushrod tubes on the right side and exposed rockers. Two carburettors were squeezed between the cylinders, angled to give a down-draught effect.

TWO-STROKES

At the end of 1935, Husqvarna quit the GP scene. In the same year, the company built its first two-stroke, a commuter bike powered by a 98cc engine with two-speed gearbox. This set a precedent for postwar production.

The two-strokes grew in capacity, and by 1960 the focus of attention was on off-road competition, notably motocross. During the following decade, the marque captured ten world motocross titles. The machine that provided the basis for this success was the 22bhp, 250cc model, developed from the 175cc, three-speed road machines of the mid-1950s.

top left The most famous and demanding of all Swedish motorcycle trials was the Novemberkåsan (November Trophy). This photograph shows the start of the 1916 event.

top During the early and mid-1930s, Husqvarna successfully raced a 497cc, 50-degree V-twin designed by Folke Mannerstedt. These three examples are shown at the 1932 Swedish Grand Prix.

above This machine was one of the first Husqvarna models. It was equipped with an imported Belgian FN single-cylinder engine, being built between 1903 and 1908.

BMW R32

BMW's first stab at a motorcycle engine was not a success. The work of Kurt Hanfland, it was a 148cc, two-stroke single, marketed under the name Flink in 1920. The Flink was followed, in 1921, by a far more substantial engine, which effectively was the true beginning of the BMW two-wheel story. Designed by Martin Stolle and designated M2B15, it was a 493cc, flat-twin side-valve with bore and stroke dimensions of 58.0x68.0mm. It was supplied to the likes of Bison, SBD, SMW, and Victoria.

In 1922, the M2B15 was used by BMW itself to power the Helios motorcycle, the engine being mounted fore-and-aft (like the British Douglas) and driving the rear wheel by chain. The Helios chassis was not a BMW design, however, even though production took place at the firm's Munich works. Unfortunately, the machine was not a very good motorcycle, a fact that led BMW's chief engineer, Max Friz (who had been responsible for the company's excellent aero engines), to put aside his personal dislike of two-wheelers and set out to create a new machine, one that BMW could be proud of.

ENTER THE R32

When the results of Friz's efforts were unveiled at the Paris Salon in October 1923, the bike caused a sensation. Its engine was mounted transversely as a single unit with a three-speed gearbox and shaft final drive, while the frame was a full twin-triangle design. The front fork was sprung by a quarter-elliptic leaf spring. It was the first BMW to carry the now-famous blue and white circular emblem (the quartering of this logo portrayed a whirling aircraft propeller and resembled Bavaria's chequered flag).

Although the R32 was not as powerful as some contemporary machines, it was superior in several important aspects. It offered a truly modern motorcycle concept at a time when unreliable engines, flimsy frames, and temperamental transmissions were commonplace.

Key features of the revolutionary design were its sprung front wheel (an industry first), its flat-twin engine, installed transversely to provide equal cooling for both cylinders, and its shaft drive to the rear wheel. Wisely, Friz decided not to far left The first BMW motorcycle to sport the famous badge, the R32 flat-twin, designed by Max Friz, made a sensational debut at the Paris Salon in October 1923.

left Production of the new R32 at BMW's Munich works, around 1924. Significantly, the work was carried out on benches, not a production line.

below R32 rider Fritz Bieber on his way to winning the 1924 German national 500cc road racing championship.

employ bevel gears to turn the drive from the crankshaft through 90 degrees, as would have been necessary with a conventional chain-drive arrangement. Instead, he opted for the simpler and mechanically more reliable shaft, which took the drive directly to the rear wheel, where a pinion meshed with a ring gear in the wheel hub.

Extremely effective, the R32 inspired subsequent generations of BMW motorcycle design. Even in the early 21st century, the same basic flat-twin engine configuration and shaft drive are employed by the German company – testament to the enduring nature of Friz's 1923 machine.

BMW R32 SPECIFICATIONS

Engine Air-cooled, side-valve, transverse, flat-twin

Displacement 494cc

Bore and stroke 68.0x68.0mm

Ignition Magneto

Gearbox Three-speed, hand-change

Final drive Shaft

Frame All-steel, welded

Dry weight 120kg (264lb)

Maximum power 8.5bhp at 3,200rpm

Top speed 90km/h (56mph)

THE USA: BIKE V. CAR

In the early years of the 20th century, the USA had a large and diverse motorcycle industry; machines from both Harley-Davidson and Indian were exported in considerable numbers to Europe. Moreover, both marques did well in racing on both sides of the Atlantic. In fact, by 1915, Indian was able to claim to be the largest manufacturer in the world, having sold a record 31,950 motorcycles that year. It is interesting to note that Indian was more advanced than Harley-Davidson in the technical stakes.

In the years leading up to World War I, the competition between Indian and Harley-Davidson produced rapid technical improvements, and not just in engines and frames. There were significant advances in transmission systems, with gear-boxes and clutches being introduced.

The war helped Harley-Davidson more than Indian, however. The former also gained considerable publicity from its famous Wrecking Crew racing team, which, from 1914 until 1921, achieved a dominant position in the American domestic racing scene.

COMPETITION FROM FOUR WHEELS

After World War I, the American motorcycle industry found itself fighting another battle – against the increasing popularity of the car, particularly in the shape of Henry Ford's Model T. The main attraction of the Model T was its bargain price, a consequence of the innovative production-line techniques used by Ford in his Detroit plant. By 1918, the Model T had already been on sale for a decade, but its real impact was felt between

that year and 1927, after which it was discontinued in favour of more modern types.

Although there was a vast increase in motorcycle sales in Europe (nearly 100 new marques appeared in Britain alone) during this period, the huge upsurge of car production in the USA, headed by the Model T, slashed the previous large number of American bike producers. Only the fittest and largest survived, marques such as Harley-Davidson, Indian, Excelsior, and Henderson.

1,200 CUBIC CENTIMETRES

From a total production of 28,189 motorcycles in 1920, Harley-Davidson's output slumped to just over 10,000 the following year. But the company didn't take this lying down and responded by launching a new, 1,200 cc, 45-degree V-twin.

As for Indian, its legendary designer Charles B. Franklin penned the 600 cc Scout, which appeared in late 1919, followed by the 1,000 cc Chief in 1922. A year later, Indian introduced the 1,200 cc Big Chief.

All of these designs were side-valve V-twins, however, and although they were basically sound machines, they often cost as much as a car and didn't change much from year to year.

Indian was purchased by E. Paul du Pont in 1930 (after suffering financial problems), while both Excelsior and Henderson folded in 1931. Quite simply, the American motorcycle industry was being left behind by its European cousin. Although both Harley-Davidson and Indian went on to survive until the post-World War II period, Indian closed in 1953.

facing page During the early years of the 20th century, the USA had a substantial and diverse motorcycle industry. Machines from the likes of Harley-Davidson (a 1914 C10 single is seen here) and Indian were exported to Europe in considerable quantities.

above left The motorcycle was widely used for police duties during the 1920s. This photograph dates from 1924 and shows how officers in Los Angeles were able to arrest offenders on the spot.

above Harley-Davidson was also very active in motorcycle sport before and immediately after World War I. Alberto Trivellato is seen here with the 1000cc V-twin he used to win the Merluzzi Hill Climb, circa 1919.

left An early 1920s Indian V-twin and sidecar.

AMERICA FLIES THE FLAG 40-41   HARLEY-DAVIDSON 160-161
HARLEY-DAVIDSON: THE MODERN ERA 204-205

THE USA: BIKE V. CAR

BROUGH SUPERIOR

Often referred to as "the Rolls Royce of motorcycles", the Brough Superior owed its existence to George Brough's father, William. The latter's foresight and enthusiasm had led to the formation of the famous Nottingham-based company.

The first all-Brough-engineered motorcycle appeared in 1902 and, thanks to its outstanding performance and handling, several examples achieved success in reliability trials. It was in this arena that George first came to prominence, riding many of the bikes to victory.

WHICH TWIN?

Despite the success of Brough machines, there was considerable disagreement between father and son in respect of the engine configuration. In 1913, George had been seen aboard a V-twin, which thereafter he favoured, whereas William Brough preferred the flat-twin (like Douglas and later BMW). In the early days, William's opinion ruled, resulting in flat-twin Broughs, but this brought George into open conflict with his father over future developments. Consequently, he set up in business on his own account, using the name Brough Superior. Quite what his father thought of this situation is best left unrecorded!

George Brough's idea was to use the very best components and technology available at the time, the results being some of the most respected motorcycles ever built. His creations were not only fast and reliable, but also good-looking and of high quality, thanks to such features as the famous Brough nickel-plated tank.

SS100

In 1924, George Brough produced his most well-known model, the legendary SS100. Each of these machines was sold with a certificate to confirm that it had reached 160 km/h (100mph) on the test track.

Basically, the SS100 was a refinement of the existing twin-camshaft, double-valve-spring SS80. It was introduced with a 988cc (85.5x86.0mm bore and stroke), overhead-valve, JAP V-twin engine and three-speed, hand-change gearbox.

The SS100 rapidly captured the public's imagination, and development continued. For 1926, the Alpine GS version was introduced, with a 995cc (80.0x99.0mm bore and stroke) JAP engine featuring triple valve springs and more power. There was also the Pendine, guaranteed to have been tested at no less than 176km/h (110mph) and named after the speed record venue on the south coast of Wales.

From 1928, rear suspension was available; but traditionalists preferred the rigid frame, as it was simpler and lighter, providing better control of the rear wheel.

A new SS100 appeared at the end of 1932. This had a JAP V-twin tuned to produce a claimed 74bhp at 6,200rpm and 200km/h (125mph). The specification included twin carburettors, twin magnetos and a selection of compression ratios, from 6:1 to 12:1 (the latter for racing only).

By the mid-1930s, a positive-stop, foot-change gearbox replaced the hand-change type; a year later, a four-speed Norton gearbox arrived. Finally, from 1936, the 50-degree, 990cc, Matchless V-twin replaced the JAP engine.

ADALBERTO GARELLI

Mention Garelli to most enthusiasts and the word "moped" would probably spring to their minds. The marque's founder, however, Adalberto Garelli, was one of the pioneers of the Italian motorcycle industry.

Garelli was born in Turin in 1886, and at the age of 22 he gained a degree in engineering, subsequently dedicating his work to the study and perfection of the first two-stroke engine at Fiat. The automobile giant did not share his enthusiasm for two-strokes, however, and he left the company in 1911.

THE SPLIT-SINGLE CONCEPT
In 1912, Garelli came up with the concept of a two-stroke split-single. It consisted of two cylinders cast in a single block, with a common combustion chamber, the two pistons working in parallel, both connected by a long gudgeon pin to a single connecting rod. Each piston had a capacity of 174.6cc, making a total of 349cc. The bore and stroke dimensions were 50.0x89.0mm.

To prove his concept, in 1914 Garelli set out to climb

Moncenisio Pass in the Alps. In succeeding, he became the first to achieve this feat on a motorcycle.

That year, Garelli also joined Bianchi as head of its motorcycle division. His next stop was Stucchi, another important motorcycle factory of the period.

During this time, he won a competition organized by the Italian Army for a military motorcycle, using a special version of his 349cc split-single. Finally, in 1919 he was able to realize a personal dream and set up his own plant, at Sesto San Giovanni, near Milan.

A VICTORIOUS DEBUT
Almost from the outset, Garelli's design attracted attention and admiration, thanks in no small part to a victorious debut in the Milano-Napoli road race. This was a remarkable success for a manufacturer that had only just begun production.

The race took place over a 840km (522-mile) route linking two of Italy's major cities. In those days, the roads were mostly of hard earth, not asphalt, but, for all that, the distance was

facing page Adalberto Garelli dedicated his life to the study and perfection of the two-stroke motorcycle engine.

left The Garelli split-single engine, showing the two pistons and their single, long connecting rod.

above A typical 1970s Garelli moped, the single-speed automatic Eureka.

below The front cover of *Moto Ciclismo*, dated 14 September 1922, showing Garelli rider Ernesto Gnesa after his victory in that month's Italian Grand Prix.

covered in 21 hours, 56 minutes, at an average speed of 38.27 km/h (23.79 mph); the rider was Ettore Girardi.

Many more victories followed over the ensuing few years; Garelli was also successful in several speed record attempts.

SEPARATE LUBRICATION

One of Garelli's 350cc racers was the first to be equipped with an oil tank for separate engine lubrication. Like the most sophisticated modern two-strokes, the oil was mixed automatically with the fuel, in a quantity that was proportioned accurately by the throttle setting. Another milestone in two-stroke technology was the use of an expansion-chamber exhaust, which used the shape of the exhaust to maximize power.

The final 1926 model of Garelli's racing 350 split-single developed 20bhp at 4,500rpm and could reach a speed of 142 km/h (88 mph). It featured a two-speed, hand-change gearbox. The oil/petrol ratio was 17 percent, and the machine weighed in (dry) at 98 kg (216 lb).

NSU: TEUTONIC MASTERCLASS

Although not the first, NSU (Neckarsulmer Strickwaren Union) was one of the real pioneering marques of the German motorcycle. It also became one of the biggest and best in that country. During the first half of the 20th century, NSU often led the world in design, innovation, and production methods, to say nothing of its sporting successes.

A WORKING PROTOTYPE

NSU was formed originally, in 1873, to manufacture and repair knitting machines. In 1900, however, it produced a prototype motorcycle equipped with a single-cylinder engine. This entered production the following year. Although sturdy, the machine was crude, its Swiss-made, Zedel clip-on engine being mounted at an incline from the frame's front downtube. Engine power was transmitted to the back wheel by a direct-drive belt, although a conventional bicycle pedal crank and chain were retained to allow the machine to be pedalled if the engine needed assistance.

Before long, NSU switched to engines of its own design, including a range of V-twins with capacities ranging from 496 to 996cc.

THE PRODUCTION LINE

The company pioneered production-line techniques for the German industry. It also took the export market seriously, opening a sales office in London during 1905.

Almost from the beginning, NSU recognized the importance of motorcycle sport as a proving ground for its technology and as a marketing tool for its products. Not only did it go racing from 1905, but it also made many successful speed record attempts over succeeding years.

Although production was switched to munitions during World War I, the firm rapidly returned to motorcycles after the conflict. By 1922, the works was operating at full capacity, with over 3,000 on the payroll.

In 1929, the famous British designer Walter Moore left Norton and joined NSU. This caused considerable controversy, his designs for the German company often being referred to as "Norton Spares Used".

TWO-STROKES

Many of Moore's NSU designs were completely original, however. One of his most successful was the 98cc, two-stroke Quick autocycle. Between 1936 and 1953, almost a quarter of a million examples were manufactured. Besides a full range of motorcycles, with capacities from 97 to 592cc, NSU built the Motosulm, essentially a moped with a 63cc, single-cylinder engine mounted over the front wheel, which it drove by chain.

The various four-stroke NSUs of the 1930s were built in side-valve, overhead-valve and overhead-camshaft forms. All were noted for their high standard of engineering and superb finish, which was often better than BMW's.

During the 1950s, NSU sold millions of machines. The company also broke more world speed records – culminating in 338km/h (210mph) in 1956 – and gained world champion-ships in the 125 and 250cc categories (1953–55).

facing page The company soon began building engines of its own design, including a range of V-twins.

above Overhead-camshaft 500 and 600cc singles were designed by Walter Moore in the mid-1930s.

right A 1938 supercharged, 345cc, double-overhead-camshaft racing twin.

below During the 1950s, NSU built the overhead-camshaft, 247cc Max and Supermax touring bikes.

below right A 1910 NSU V-twin with early rear suspension.

FOOT-CHANGE GEARBOX

In the very early years of the motorcycle, drive was taken directly from the engine shaft to the driven wheel, usually by means of a belt. As a result, there was no way of isolating the wheel from the shocks and irregularities of the torque delivered by the engine. At first, manufacturers looked at improving the flexibility and smoothness of the engine, hence the comparatively large number of multi-cylinder engines introduced so early in the history of the motorcycle. Twin- and four-cylinder examples began to appear almost as soon as the motorcycle was invented.

PEDAL ASSISTED

Nevertheless, the problems of intractability remained, and the belt did nothing to diminish them. This was also a reason why many early machines were equipped with pedals, which could be used when starting off, stopping, climbing hills and the like.

Then, during the first decade of the 20th century, two-speed transmissions appeared in the de Dion-Bouton, Fafnir, NSU, Royal Enfield, and Scott, while Chater-Lea introduced a three-speed gearbox as early as 1906. There was also a variable-ratio pulley system devised by Rudge-Whitworth for its famous Rudge Multi model (a similar system was used on the Zenith Gradua).

THE BIG BREAKTHROUGH

While all-chain drive (primary and final), primary gears, and shaft final drive came as by-products of the gearbox and clutch mechanisms, there still remained the relatively slow and complicated (with levers, rods, and joints) hand-operation. For a long time, control of the gearbox was by a hand lever, which moved through a quadrant to provide a progressive sequence of gear selection. The rider's hands were already pretty well occupied, however, so it was clearly desirable to transfer some of these duties to his feet. Using a pedal to change gear was an attractive concept, but it was not compatible with the quadrant type of progressive change, which required more sensitivity than a heavily booted foot could achieve.

The problem was solved by Velocette chief designer Harold Willis in 1928, when his positive-stop mechanism was introduced on the works TT model. It soon became standard on Velocette's production KTT racer.

With the positive-stop system, the gear lever no longer moved to a separate position for each gear, but was simply prodded to engage the next highest or lowest gear. Then, it would spring back to its original position.

Soon, other manufacturers began employing positive-stop operation. Later, four-speed gearboxes replaced the two- and three-speed types. Five, and sometimes six, ratios arrived in the 1960s, having first been used in racing. In the 1970s, Honda and Moto Guzzi introduced models with automatic gear-boxes, but these proved unpopular and were soon dropped.

TRIUMPH SPEED TWIN

Edward Turner's Speed Twin was one of the truly great motorcycle designs of the 20th century. Launched at the end of July 1937, it not only propelled Triumph into the big league, but also made the traditional big singles and V-twins seem old hat.

A SIMPLE DESIGN

As with all great designs, the Speed Twin was essentially simple. Amazingly, the engine was actually lighter and narrower than the Tiger 90 single of the same era. Turner could have built a flat-twin (like BMW and Douglas) or a V-twin (like JAP and Matchless), but chose a vertical layout because it offered the prospect of the best power-to-weight ratio, the layout making it possible to design a compact assembly. Other reasons, as Turner explained, included "…even firing intervals, perfect cooling, and extreme rigidity, which is the essence of high power output; the engine will go into a smaller frame without loss of accessibility; the two cylinders do precisely the same amount of work, and the engine is amenable to all single-cylinder tuning techniques… This type of engine is superior to any other form of twin except on balance."

OVERHEAD VALVES

At first, Turner had planned an overhead-camshaft layout, but this was soon abandoned in favour of a twin-camshaft, pushrod design with overhead valves. The arrangement was pleasingly symmetrical, the gear-driven camshafts being positioned fore and aft of the cylinder barrels.

A valuable aspect of Edward Turner's design genius was his ability to utilize existing components to minimize production costs. A good example of this was the 498.76cc displacement of the new Speed Twin, which was based on identical 63.0x80.0mm bore and stroke dimensions to Triumph's Tiger 70 250 single. Thus, production could be rationalized by employing the same pistons, rings, small-ends, and circlips.

ORIGINAL FEATURES

Even so, several features of the new Triumph engine were original. One was the patented built-up crankshaft, which had no middle bearing. There were also light-alloy connecting rods. Another patented construction was the big-end. This was unusual in several respects. Each cylinder's con-rod bore directly on its crankpin, but the steel bearing cap featured a thin lining of white metal. This arrangement took advantage of the high heat conductivity of the alloy, while the white-metalled cap acted as a safety feature because, in the event of oil loss, the metal would melt, preventing seizure.

Coded 5T, the Speed Twin was built until the late 1950s in its original form, with separate gearbox. A unit-construction (combined engine and gearbox) version was introduced, as the 5TA, for 1959; it was offered until the end of 1966.

1937 TRIUMPH SPEED TWIN
SPECIFICATIONS

Engine Air-cooled, overhead-valve, vertical twin

Displacement 499cc

Bore and stroke 63.0x80.0mm

Ignition Magneto

Gearbox Four-speed, foot-change

Final drive Chain

Frame All-steel, tubular construction

Dry weight 160kg (353lb)

Maximum power 26bhp at 6,000rpm

Top speed 145km/h (90mph)

facing page A 1949 Triumph advertisement, proclaiming the virtues of the Speed Twin and the fact that the design had a ten-year start over its rivals.

left A 1946 5T Speed Twin, with front-mounted dynamo, the first postwar Triumph.

below Edward Turner's Speed Twin was one of the truly great motorcycles of the 20th century. Launched in July 1937, it started a fashion for vertical twins that other manufacturers would follow.

4 THE POSTWAR BOOM

above left Almost 25,000 German Dürkopp Diana scooters were built between 1954 and 1960. Its single-cylinder, two-stroke engine displaced 194 cc.

left Introduced in 1950, the German Horex Regina was powered by a 342 cc, four-stroke single with pushrod-operated valves and twin exhaust ports.

above During the immediate postwar period, motorcycles were widely used not only for commuting, but also for touring, as these Italians prove during a visit to Britain on their 250 cc Comet in 1956.

right A 1950s British Triumph 500 cc Speed Twin, capturing the carefree spirit of the day.

THE POSTWAR BOOM

After the end of World War II in 1945, the world's motorcycle manufacturers enjoyed a sales boom that lasted until the end of the 1950s.

Initially, the world market was split into three distinct areas: Continental Europe, North America, and Britain. In Europe, the emphasis was on cheap transport, and there was an enlightened attitude to mopeds – no test or insurance was required for machines under 50 cc with pedals. This helped establish a two-wheel culture based on mopeds, scooters, and lightweight motorcycles. In North America, the population was wealthier, and many large-capacity roadsters and dirt bikes were bought as fun

vehicles. In Britain, the economy was in such a poor state that for the rest of the 1940s, every machine produced had to go for export to help pay off the nation's debts incurred during six long years of war.

Peak motorcycle sales were achieved during the 1950s, when many new designs were introduced, notably from Germany, Italy, and Britain. Manufacturers in Spain, France, and Sweden also built relatively large numbers of machines. The American domestic motorcycle industry stagnated, however, and Harley-Davidson was the only company that managed to survive in the long term.

There were several important developments during the

1945–59 period. Besides the growth in moped and scooter sales, a number of new 500, 650, and 700 cc, twin-cylinder models were introduced by British manufacturers. Technical advances included suspension improvements (the telescopic front fork and swinging-arm rear with twin hydraulically damped shock absorbers), the dualseat, 12-volt electrics, and push-button starting on some German designs.

There was also a vibrant motorcycle industry behind the Iron Curtain. East Germany produced IFA (later MZ) and Simson machines; Czechoslovakia, Jawa, and CZ; Poland, WSK, and Junak. The Soviet Union turned out copies of pre-war German DKW and BMW designs.

Although everything seemed fine in the world motor-cycle market, there were problems, and they were serious. For a start, the founding fathers of the industry – the pioneers – men such as the Collier brothers, Carlo Guzzi, and Edward Turner were growing old. In addition, steadily rising standards of living toward the end of the 1950s meant that, for the first time, many potential customers could afford a small car. Then there was the growing challenge from the Far East, where the Japanese had been working hard to build a vast industry, which would provide serious competition for the West in the 1960s.

above This 1958 BSA A7 Shooting Star, with its 497cc, overhead-valve, vertical twin engine and separate gearbox, is typical of the British motorcycle industry's products immediately after World War II.

BRITISH INDUSTRY

Although the British had been on the winning side, when World War II ended in 1945, the nation was at a low ebb financially; the years of conflict had taken a fearsome toll on the country's economy. Thus, even though there was a ready-made home market waiting to buy its products, the British motorcycle industry was forced to sell everything it could produce overseas, prompted by Sir Stafford Cripps' call to British industry in his 1945 budget speech: "Export or bust!"

RAISING TARGETS

Where motorcycles were concerned, Cripps had demanded that, by 1948, export figures be raised to a staggering 258 percent of the 1938 level. The manufacturers responded by achieving 278 percent by 1947. Some industry suppliers also took part in this export drive, including Lucas (electrical equipment), Smiths (instruments), and Amal (carburettors).

The main overseas markets were the USA, Canada, Australia, and Europe. In fact, it would be true to say that such names as BSA, Norton, and Triumph became as well-known

abroad as at home during the immediate postwar period. Triumph, in particular, carved a reputation in North America to rival the domestic Harley-Davidson and Indian brands.

THE MARQUES

At the time, Britain seemed to have an almost endless list of manufacturers. The major companies were AMC (AJS and Matchless), the BSA Group (BSA, Triumph, Sunbeam, and Ariel), Douglas, Norton, Panther, Royal Enfield, Velocette, and Vincent. There were scores of smaller marques, too, such as Cotton, DMW, DOT, Excelsior, Francis-Barnett, James, New Hudson, Scott, and Sun.

BEST-SELLERS

BSA not only controlled the most powerful grouping, but at that time was also the best-selling brand in the world. From its giant plant in Small Heath, Birmingham, came its established B31 and B33 singles, together with new twins in the shape of the 497cc A7 and 646cc A10 models. Later, the company left P & M (Panther) was a Yorkshire firm that had built its first motorcycle in 1904. The company's machines are seen here at an exhibition in Copenhagen, Denmark, in 1951.

below left Matchless was based in south-east London and belonged to the AMC (Associated Motor Cycles) Group. By 1957, this also included the AJS, Norton, James, and Francis-Barnett marques.

below A police-specification Matchless G12 646cc twin on patrol with London's Metropolitan force, circa 1962.

bottom During the 1950s, the Automobile Association's sturdy, side-valve BSA M21 and box sidecar outfits were common sights on British roads.

developed high-performance versions, including the Gold Star, Shooting Star, Road Rocket, Super Rocket, and, finally, the Rocket Gold Star.

Another member of the group, Triumph, had introduced the trend-setting Speed Twin model in the late 1930s, which was joined in late 1949 by the 649cc Thunderbird. Like their BSA counterparts, there were high-performance versions of these machines, among them the Tiger 100, Tiger 110, and T120 Bonneville.

Ariel (also a major brand within the BSA Group) built both 500 and 650cc vertical twins, as did rivals Norton, AJS, Matchless, and Royal Enfield. All of these marques produced large numbers of single-cylinder machines as well, often updated prewar models.

Most British motorcycles of the 1940s and 1950s featured separate engines and gearboxes. From the beginning of the 1960s, however, some firms, notably BSA and Triumph, switched to unit construction, where the engine, gearbox, and clutch were combined in a single assembly.

TRIUMPH SPEED TWIN 76-77
CAFE RACER CULTURE 108-109

THE SCOOTER AGE

Although the first scooters appeared shortly after World War I, the golden era for sales ran from the mid-1940s to the mid-1960s, when they met a demand for inexpensive personal transport. At the beginning of the 21st century, however, a new breed of these small-wheeled machines began to appear, this time aimed at providing mobility with style.

THE ITALIANS SET THE PACE

Immediately after World War II, the Italian aircraft maker Piaggio and engineering giant Innocenti almost put their entire country back on wheels with their respective Vespa and Lambretta scooters.

Prohibited from building aircraft, in 1945 Piaggio created a small monocoque machine. Its design was so advanced that its shape and engineering principles would form the basis of all Vespa scooters sold over the next 50 years or so. Originally displacing 98cc, it evolved through 125 and 150cc versions before being given a 200cc engine. Vespa never deviated from its original concept of a monocoque body shell with the engine mounted inside and adjacent to the rear wheel.

By contrast, the Lambretta retained its tubular frame, having either shaft or fully enclosed chain final drive.

DOUGLAS AND NSU

The vast sales enjoyed by the Vespa and Lambretta soon attracted attention abroad and, in 1949, the Bristol-based Douglas company announced its intention to build a version of the former. The British company made a number of changes to the Piaggio design, one of which was the relocation of the headlamp from its original position on the front mudguard to the front apron, to meet UK law.

In Germany, NSU purchased a licence to build the Lambretta LC in 1951. This had been the Italian marque's first model to feature enclosed bodywork, having been introduced a year earlier.

When NSU's licence expired, the company created the Prima series, the first model being launched at the Brussels motorcycle show in January 1956. Although, at first glance, the Prima D appeared similar to the Lambretta LC, in fact, it was much improved. It was a true luxury scooter, with an electric starter and a new, hydraulic, rear shock absorber.

THE GERMAN INDUSTRY RESPONDS

While the British industry never really followed Douglas's lead to mass-produce scooters, the Germans did. After NSU's Prima came a host of innovative luxury models, including the TWN Contessa, Maico Mobil, and Maicoletta, Dürkopp Diana, Heinkel Tourist, and Zündapp Bella.

Heinkel had also been an aircraft manufacturer, and in 1952, unable to continue in this field, it began building the Tourist. This had a 174cc, overhead-valve, four-stroke, fan-cooled engine. It was quiet, powerful, and comfortable. A tubular frame supported steel body panels and cast-aluminium footboards, while the engine was rubber mounted to eliminate vibration. As one commentator put it at the time, "If the Heinkel were a car, it would truly be deserving of executive status."

left Lambretta and rival Vespa were the most successful of all scooter marques. This is Lambretta's LD150, built between 1954 and 1958.

facing page:
top Like Piaggio, Heinkel put its aviation engineering expertise into scooters. The result was the high-quality Tourist.

bottom left The 1959 Iso Milano had a 150cc engine.

bottom right Zündapp, one of Germany's premier motorcycle marques, built the Bella scooter. The R203 had a 197cc, single-cylinder, two-stroke engine and could reach 93km/h (58mph).

Milano Model
Complete with saver borders and rear side panel grilles.
Retail Price
£166 - 19 - 6
Including Purchase Tax

Iso

The 150 cc. 4 speed scooter

ISO s.p.a. AUTOMOTOVEICOLI · BRESSO (Milano)

Bella
R 203

Man kann sich damit sehen lassen!

The stylish sports moped and light weight motorcycle

Les vélomoteurs sportifs de rasse et motocyclettes légères

El gallardo velomotor deportivo y la arrojada motocicleta ligera

MOPEDS

Most early motorcycles were motorized bicycles and, in the 1920s, this simple form of machine was developed to become the autocycle, the forerunner of the moped. Unlike the true moped, which invariably had an engine of 50cc or less, the autocycle was usually around 100cc.

CLIP-ONS

Immediately after World War II, the "clip-on" appeared, being an engine that was simply clipped to a conventional pedal cycle frame. Leading manufacturers included Garelli, Power Pak, and Ducati, the last being the most interesting technically. Called the Cucciolo, it had a four-stroke engine, which gave it a distinct advantage over the two-stroke opposition.

The Cucciolo's valves were operated by pullrods, rather than pushrods, and it had an integral two-speed, pre-selector gearbox and all-metal clutch. Launched in 1945, the engine unit, exhaust, and fuel tank were supplied as a kit for the customer to fit to an existing pedal cycle.

THE U-FRAME MOPED

By the early 1950s, several manufacturers, including NSU, Mobylette, Zündapp, Heinkel, and Ducati, were offering complete machines, using specially-made U-frame structures.

The two most interesting designs were both German: the NSU Quickly and Heinkel Perle. The first Quickly, the N,

appeared in 1953; when production ceased in 1962, almost 540,000 had been manufactured – the total for all variants of the Quickly is an amazing 1.2 million!

Powered by a 49cc, piston-port, two-stroke single, the NSU offered a combination of simple style, quality, and low price. By contrast, the Heinkel Perle (also introduced in 1953) was very advanced, being the first of such small machines to have a cast-alloy frame and swinging-arm rear suspension. A high price restricted sales. Other major U-frame mopeds included the Japanese Honda Graduate and PC50, French Mobylette, Austrian Puch Maxi, and Italian Vespa Ciao.

SPORTS MODELS

The next stage in the evolution of the moped was the sports model. In reality, this was a miniature motorcycle, but with a 50cc engine and pedals. Early examples included the German Victoria Avanti (1959) and Ducati 48 Sport (1963). In the 1970s, high-performance examples appeared, including the Garelli Rekord and Tiger Cross, Yamaha FS1E, Suzuki API, Malaguti Calvacone, and Gilera Touring and Trail. Eventually, legislation was imposed to limit performance, and a more practical kickstarter replaced the awkward pedal starting.

Sales of all mopeds declined as the 1980s dawned, their place being taken in the 1990s by a new breed of 50cc automatic scooter.

below Ducati's Cucciolo was a clip-on engine kit for motorizing a pedal cycle. The name means "little pup" in Italian.

facing page The German Victoria Avanti was designed toward the end of the 1950s. It was an early attempt at providing a sports moped, a genre that would peak in popularity during the 1970s.

above From the early 1960s, the Japanese Honda company built mopeds for the European market at a new production facility in Belgium. Typical was the Graduate; this is a 1973 model.

below The Malaguti 49 cc Calvacone, an enduro-styled ultra-lightweight motorcycle, was built in the mid-1970s. It was offered with pedals in several countries, to qualify as a moped.

EDWARD TURNER

Born in London on 24 January 1901, a few hours after the death of Queen Victoria, Edward Turner was given his Christian name because he was the first true Edwardian of seven children – he had three sisters and three brothers. His father owned a light-engineering business, so with this background it comes as no surprise to learn that Edward set up his own motorcycle dealership in south London. Subsequently, he was head-hunted during the late 1920s by Charles Sangster, then boss of the Birmingham-based Ariel company.

A MOVE TO TRIUMPH

At Ariel, Turner designed the legendary Square Four. During the early 1930s, Jack Sangster succeeded his father and subsequently acquired the Triumph marque. He moved Edward Turner to his new acquisition, installing him as managing director and chief designer. Turner's first creation for Triumph

was the range of Tiger singles (250, 350, and 500cc), which amply demonstrated his outstanding styling prowess. Quite simply, he had taken the existing Triumph overhead-valve singles, which had been designed by Valentine Page, and equipped them with tuned engines and additional brightwork. The latter included chromed tank panels, while the remaining body parts were finished with silver paintwork. The transformation turned them into best-sellers.

In 1937, Turner's most famous creation, the Speed Twin, was introduced. It was followed a year later by its more highly tuned brother, the Tiger 100. These two models, equipped with the same 500cc, parallel-twin engine, really cemented his reputation within the industry.

During World War II, the original Triumph factory in Coventry was destroyed by bombing, but a new facility was built a few miles away, in the village of Meriden.

facing page, top left The headlamp nacelle was a Turner styling feature.

left For 1963, Turner and his team revamped the long-running Triumph vertical twin, creating the new unit-construction range of 649cc models, including the 6T Thunderbird.

above A Triumph brochure from 1951, showing the 6T Thunderbird (foreground) and 5T Speed Twin.

above right A 1960 Triumph T120 Bonneville. This model, with the pre-unit engine, was an icon of the 1960s biking scene.

right Edward Turner (right) with Bill Johnson (American West Coast Triumph importer), outside Triumph's factory at Meriden, July 1948.

THE THUNDERBIRD

In late September 1949, Turner's next significant design made its debut, the 649cc (71.0x82.0mm bore and stroke) Thunderbird. It was launched in a blaze of publicity, the first three production models being taken to the Montlhéry circuit in France, where they covered 800km (500 miles), finishing with a flying lap at over 160km/h (100mph).

A brand-new Triumph single appeared in November 1952. This was the 149cc (57.0x58.5mm bore and stroke), overhead-valve, unit-construction Terrier. From the Terrier came the 199cc (63.0x64.0mm bore and stroke) Tiger Cub, which was introduced in 1953 and remained in production until the late 1960s.

The twin-cylinder range received the Tiger 110 (the sports version of the Thunderbird) for 1954, followed by the even quicker T120 Bonneville for 1959. The 3TA Twenty One was the first unit-construction Triumph twin, being launched in 1957; eventually, all Triumph twins followed this route.

Turner did have the occasional failure, however, such as his sprung-hub rear suspension, which appeared in the immediate postwar period.

Turner's other great gift was his ability to manage costs – his designs made money, which ensured that his time as the company's boss (postwar until the mid-1960s) was Triumph's most successful period. He died on 15 August 1973.

GERMAN DESIGN

Following World War II and the division of Germany, there were distinct differences in the motorcycle designs that came from companies in the West and East.

THE WEST

In West Germany, civilian motorcycle production did not resume seriously until 1947. At that time, the standard of living of the majority of the population was barely above subsistence level. Not surprisingly, the early postwar machines tended to be simple utility models. In the early 1950s, however, the accent switched to technical innovation, performance, and luxury features, all of which reflected the massive improvement in living standards. By the mid-1950s, West Germany's economic revival was in full swing. The main West German motorcycle marques of the era were Adler, BMW, DKW, Hercules, Horex, NSU, TWN, Victoria, and Zündapp.

Like many West German manufacturers, Adler specialized in two-stroke engines, although the bikes had unusual transmission systems. The 200 and 250cc twins featured an engine-speed clutch mounted on the crankshaft, outside the primary drive, which was by helical gears. The 98 and 125cc singles employed an even more unusual layout, however, the engine being offset to the right, and the clutch and gearbox to the left. Drive to the rear wheel was taken from a sprocket adjacent to the clutch, between the engine and gearbox and concentric with the crankshaft. This was unique to Adler.

NSU offered the Max and Super Max. Displacing 247cc, these overhead-camshaft singles featured a type of valve gear that was unique among motorcycles. Designed by Albert Roder and called Ultramax, the overhead valve gear was driven by long connecting rods, which were housed in a tunnel cast integrally on the left side of the cylinder barrel.

Of all the West German marques, however, Victoria was the most innovative. It produced not only the 347cc Bergmeister narrow-angle, transverse V-twin (introduced in 1951), but also the 197cc Swing. Hailed at its 1956 launch as revolutionary, the Swing was the first motorcycle to have push-button gear changing. It also featured a unique form of

BDG 250 L
with double-piston engine

facing page Launched in 1934, the Zündapp K800 had a flat-four engine displacing 804cc. Weighing in at 212kg (467lb), it could reach 125km/h (78mph).

left The German Triumph marque (known as TWN – Triumph Werke Nurnburg – in many countries) produced a series of excellent two-stroke models during the 1950s, including the BDG 250 (shown) and Boss 350 split-singles.

below The BMW 500cc R50 and 600cc R69 models were launched at the Brussels Salon in January 1955. Both featured Earles forks and swinging-arm rear suspension.

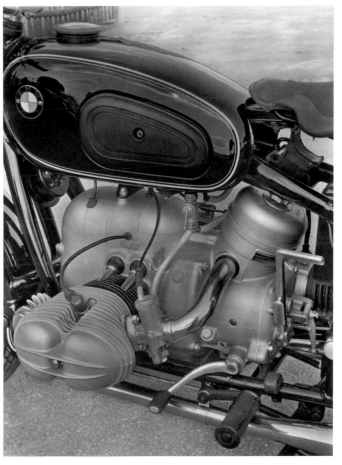

rear wheel and engine suspension, the engine assembly being pivoted from the frame below the crankcase.

THE EAST

By the late 1950s, the West German motorcycle industry was in decline, its customer base having melted away to purchase cars. In the communist-controlled East, however, there were no such problems. State-owned MZ and Simson enjoyed stability for many decades until the Berlin Wall came down in 1989. At that point, they suffered the same fate as the West German motorcycle industry some three decades before.

Prior to that, both marques had built millions of small-capacity, piston-port-induction, two-stroke, single-cylinder models. Although basic in overall concept, these had been in high demand throughout the old Soviet Empire. In stark contrast, MZ had also produced technically advanced racers, designed by the brilliant engineer Walter Kaaden.

SPANISH STARS

No European country changed so dramatically during the second half of the 20th century as Spain. From a rural, pre-industrial society ruled by a Fascist dictator, Spain became a modern, thrusting democracy and an integral part of the European Community.

THE BEGINNING OF AN INDUSTRY

The Spanish Civil War (1936–39), which had been won by General Franco's Nationalists, left Spain a divided nation. Unlike most European nations, however, it managed to escape involvement in World War II. And it was during this period that the Spanish took their first hesitant steps toward modernization – and the creation of a domestic motorcycle industry.

The first two companies, Montesa and Sanglas, had already laid the foundations prior to the end of the war in Europe (spring 1945), giving them a head start over the international competition. General Franco's government did the rest by imposing stringent import bans on foreign vehicles and associated components.

MONTESA AND SANGLAS

By the end of the 1940s, Montesa (founded by Pedro Permanyer and Francisco Bulto) was building a range of single-cylinder, two-stroke machines and competing in grand prix racing. Sanglas, meanwhile, was producing 350 and 500cc, overhead-valve, unit-construction engines. The company also became an early user of the hydraulically damped, telescopic front fork.

EXPANSION

It was during the 1950s, however, that expansion of the industry really took off. This was prompted by the arrival of Derbi, Ossa, and a host of other minor marques, their machines often being powered by Hispano-Villiers engines (British Villiers designs built under licence in Spain).

By the end of the decade, the major players had been joined by Bultaco and Mototrans, the latter producing Italian Ducatis under licence.

FRANCISCO BULTO

The most well-known of all Spanish designers was Francisco Bulto, co-founder of Montesa, who left the company in the spring of 1958 to form his own brand, Bultaco. In time, this became Spain's most influential and most sporting marque.

Bultaco's first design, a 125cc, two-stroke street bike led to an excellent series of roadsters, the TSS range of racers (built in 125, 196, 250, and 350cc guises) and, most significantly, a range of world-beating motocross, trials, and enduro bikes. The Sherpa trials bike, for example, developed with the assistance of legendary rider Sammy Miller, changed the face of one-day events when it appeared in the mid-1960s. Overnight, the previously dominant, big four-stroke singles became obsolete. Moreover, there is absolutely no doubt that Bultaco's success encouraged its rivals, Montesa and Ossa, to follow suit, thus creating a new "Spanish Armada" which, this time, was successful.

facing page, left In 1946, Simeon Rabasa Singla's Derbi company built its first motorcycle; in 1969, the marque won the 50cc world championship, the first of many successes.

facing page, right Manuel Giro and, later, his son, Eduardo, were responsible for the successes gained by Ossa. This Phantom 250 motocrosser dates from the 1970s.

above One of Bultaco's best-known bikes was the Sherpa trials machine, which appeared in 1965.

right A mid-1960s Montesa brochure illustration, showing (left to right) the Sport 250, Impala 175 and 60cc Micro.

SPORTING LIGHTWEIGHTS

Before the arrival of the Japanese in the world motorcycle market during the 1960s, European manufacturers largely led the industry. This was certainly the case when it came to features such as mechanical innovation, design practices, and variety of engine types (both four-stroke and two-stroke). And without doubt, the Italians were the style kings.

THE ITALIANS MAKE THE RUNNING
As with scooters, Italy made the running in the field of sporting lightweight motorcycles. There were various reasons for this. One was that the Italians had been able to resume production more rapidly than anyone else after World War II because, of the major marques, only Benelli's factory at Pesaro on the Adriatic coast had been extensively damaged during the conflict. Several brand-new designs appeared at the first post-war Milan motorcycle show, in December 1946.

Another reason for Italian dominance of the lightweight market was the nation's love of speed events. While the basic requirement was for everyday transport, a model with a racing pedigree, stylish looks, and a bit of excitement was, in the Italian designer's mind, likely to sell in larger numbers than a dull looker, no matter how well engineered, comfortable, and practical. The latter priorities served manufacturers well in Great Britain, Germany, and Scandinavia, but not red-blooded Italy. Long-distance road events, such as the Giro d'Italia (Tour of Italy) and Milano-Taranto, plus the Italian Formula 2 and 3 racing series, also proved breeding grounds for high-performance, lightweight sports bikes.

THE RIVALS
Immediately after World War II, the established Italian marques, such as Bianchi, Moto Guzzi, and Gilera, had been joined by a host of newcomers. Some of these were large organizations that had built aircraft previously, but had been prohibited from doing so by the Allies following the conflict – Aermacchi (Macchi), Capriolo (Caproni), MV Agusta (Agusta), and Vespa (Piaggio). While the last of these concentrated on scooters, the other companies produced motorcycles, as did another major military supplier, Ducati, which had built radios and electrical equipment.

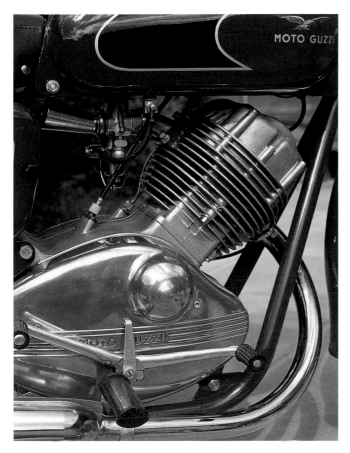

below Another notable Italian lightweight was the Aermacchi overhead-valve single with horizontal cylinder. This 175 cc Ala Rossa dates from 1961.

bottom Compared with Italian lightweights, British machines looked much heavier. This is a 250 cc 1965 Matchless G2 CSR.

facing page Besides its legendary overhead-camshaft singles, Ducati built a family of small-capacity, pushrod singles, including this 1957 98 cc Sport. Note the unusual oil cooler ahead of the crankcase.

above Carlo Guzzi's last design, the 1956 Lodola, a 175 cc, overhead-camshaft single. Of particular interest was its inclined cylinder and heel/toe gearchange with indicator.

INNOVATIVE DESIGN

Although the established firms built some good machines – for example, the Bianchi Tonale (175cc), Moto Guzzi Lodola (175 and 235cc), and Gilera 125/150cc models – the newcomers really made the running with their offerings. These benefited not only from a "clean sheet" when it came to design and styling, but also from the wealth of engineering talent that was at the disposal of the companies. The results were some true classics, among them the Aermacchi Ala Rossa (175cc) and Ala Verde (250cc); the MV Agusta Disco Volante (Flying Saucer); and the Ducati 98 Sport, 175 Sport, and 200 Elite. Technically, however, Capriolo was probably the most interesting marque, with its three main designs. The first of these was a 150cc flat-twin (BMW style); the second a 75cc, face-cam design, in which the crankshaft ran in line with the pressed-steel frame; the third retained the face-cam layout, but with a more conventional bottom end.

SIDECARS

Almost as soon as the motorcycle was accepted as a serious means of transportation – rather than simply an experimental "toy" – riders wanted to carry passengers. This was achieved by attaching a sidecar.

The Oakley Motor Company is said to have invented the sidecar as early as 1900; within three to four years, development was being undertaken by several concerns. There was some debate initially as to whether a rigidly or flexibly mounted sidecar was the most practical, but eventually the former became almost universal practice. At the time, most sidecar bodies were made of wicker to minimize weight, being little more than an upholstered seat with a protective apron for the passenger.

FAMILY TRANSPORT

Following World War I, there was a strong demand for motorized transport for the family. As a result, many specialist sidecar manufacturers came into being, while many motorcycle producers began offering their own "chairs". In Britain, these included BSA, Matchless, Royal Enfield, Sunbeam, Douglas, Panther, Ariel, Chater-Lea, and Triumph. Of the many Continental European sidecar manufacturers, the two most important marques were German: BMW and Steib.

During the 1920s, many families acquired a sidecar outfit simply to save money, and sidecar design evolved. Whereas the first models were nearly all single-seaters, child-and-adult and finally full double-adult versions followed.

For weather protection, sidecars were fitted with simple windscreens at first, but folding hoods and finally hard tops soon followed. Steel or aluminium was employed subsequently for the bodywork.

The sidecar was also used during this period as an alternative to a light van, manufacturers offering models designed specifically for various trades. The sidecar outfit began to be used in sporting events as well, not only for the likes of hill climbs and trials, but also grand prix racing.

By 1936, there were half a million motorcycles on British roads, of which no fewer than 25 percent hauled sidecars.

THE SIDECAR'S HEYDAY

The sidecar's real heyday, however, was in the immediate post-war period of the late 1940s and throughout the 1950s. At the end of World War II in 1945, established sidecar manufacturers returned to the business with renewed energy. Increased demand also led to many new companies being formed, among them Busmar, Blacknell, and Garrard.

In the mid-1950s, the new plastic material, glass-fibre, began to be employed. One of the first sidecars to enter production using this material was the Watsonian Bambini, a single-seater for lightweight motorcycles and scooters.

In the early 1960s, however, sidecar sales began a slide from which they never recovered. There were two main reasons: the prevalence of sporting motorcycles, many of which were not suitable for a third wheel, and the advent of the affordable small car, such as the legendary Mini.

facing page, left Watsonian was the biggest and most well-known of all British sidecar manufacturers. The company's 1954 catalogue detailed touring, racing, and trials models.

facing page, right A familiar sight on the roads of Europe during the 1950s – a motor-cycle and double-adult sidecar. In this case, a 1958 Panther 100 (600cc) and San Remo "chair".

above The 1960 World Sidecar Champions Helmut Fath (driver) and Alfred Wohlgemuth, racing in the Isle of Man TT with their BMW Rennsport 500cc outfit.

right Also pictured in 1960, a Royal Enfield 692cc Constellation and Watsonian New Monark sports sidecar.

VINCENT HRD

The Vincent HRD V-twin has gained a special place in motor-cycle history, thanks to such famous models as the Rapide, Black Shadow, and Black Lightning. Philip Conrad Vincent, known simply as PCV, acquired the HRD motorcycle brand from its founder, Howard Raymond Davies, in 1927.

THE INFLUENCE OF PHIL IRVING

In 1932, PCV hired the Australian Phil Irving as chief designer, the pair famously designing the first brand-new model (a 500cc, overhead-valve single) in a hectic 11-week period. This made its debut at London's Olympia motorcycle show in 1934. The legendary motorcycles that followed are generally agreed to have been the fruits of both men's labour and design skills.

It was Irving, however, who came up with the idea of a V-twin. This had been prompted one day at Vincent's Stevenage works, where he had seen a drawing of the 500cc engine lying on top of another so that the crankcases overlapped.

With funds always in short supply, the concept had distinct possibilities. Although a new crankcase would be needed,

existing barrels, heads, con-rods, timing gear, gearbox, and other components could be utilized without major change.

THE SERIES A RAPIDE

The prototype of what would become the Series A Rapide (nicknamed the "plumber's nightmare" because of its plethora of fuel and oil pipes) made its public debut in October 1936. It sported a 47.5-degree, V-twin engine with short pushrods operating overhead valves. Displacing 998cc (84.0x90.0mm bore and stroke), this was claimed to produce 45bhp at 5,500rpm. Only 78 examples were built before production ceased in July 1939 as Britain prepared for Hitler's war.

THE SERIES B RAPIDE

Compared with the limited-production prewar model, the post-war Series B Rapide was a much better bike. The engine was considerably different, having a wider 50-degree angle between the cylinders, even though the same bore and stroke dimensions were used. The valve gear was enclosed, while a

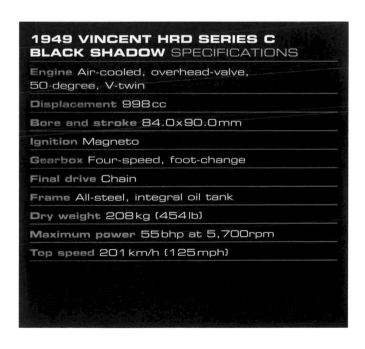

facing page Created by Philip
Vincent and Phil Irving, the
original, Series A 998cc Vincent
HRD employed a 47.5-degree
V-twin engine. Postwar, as on
this 1950s Series C Rapide,
the V angle was increased to
50 degrees.

left A stately setting for a
stately motorcycle: a 1950 499
cc Vincent Comet single. Essentially, the machine's engine was
half a V-twin.

change had been made from hairpin to coil valve springs. In
addition, the prewar design had suffered from gearbox and
clutch problems, so these had been replaced by new items.

Another major alteration was that the top tube of the
frame had been axed in favour of a one-piece, 16-gauge steel
oil tank incorporated into a backbone that ran from the
steering head to the dualseat.

THE BLACK SHADOW AND SERIES C

The prototype of the Black Shadow sports model appeared in
early 1948, Vincent claiming that it was capable of 201 km/h
(125 mph). Later that year, the Series C was introduced
in both Rapide and Black Shadow forms.

A major difference between the B and C series was that
the former employed the prewar Brampton girder front fork,
whereas the "C" had the new Girdraulic fork, which was
claimed to be superior to even the telescopic type. The fork
blades were manufactured from heat-treated forgings of L40
alloy by the Bristol Aircraft Company.

1949 VINCENT HRD SERIES C BLACK SHADOW SPECIFICATIONS

Engine Air-cooled, overhead-valve,
50-degree, V-twin

Displacement 998cc

Bore and stroke 84.0x90.0mm

Ignition Magneto

Gearbox Four-speed, foot-change

Final drive Chain

Frame All-steel, integral oil tank

Dry weight 208kg (454lb)

Maximum power 55bhp at 5,700rpm

Top speed 201km/h (125mph)

COMMUTER BIKES

Today, the role of personal transport has been neatly filled by the small car, and it may be difficult to believe that much of Western Europe went to work and play on myriad small-capacity, mainly two-stroke-engined, motorcycles during the period immediately after World War II. That, however, is exactly what took place.

Britain, Germany, France, Spain, and Italy all produced suitable designs. Often, these small machines were powered by bought-in engines, from such manufacturers as Villiers (British), Ilo and Sachs (German), and Minerelli and Franco Morini (Italian). Villiers engines were also manufactured under licence in other countries, including Spain.

BRITAIN

Among the most popular British commuter bikes were the various BSA Bantam models (125, 150, and 175cc). The Bantam first appeared in 1948 as the D1, its 123cc engine being an obvious copy of the German DKW RT125; the last B175 model left the production line in March 1971.

The origins of the Royal Enfield two-stroke series could also be traced back to the DKW. There was a wide range of models, stretching from the wartime 126cc ML to the 148cc Prince, production of which finally ceased in 1962.

Although the BSA and Royal Enfield models had employed "in-house" engines, the vast majority of British commuter bikes used Villiers engines. The most important of these machines came from Ambassador, Excelsior, Francis-Barnett, Greeves, James, Norman, and Sun.

GERMANY

Like Britain, the West German motorcycle industry – as opposed to that of the communist-controlled Eastern zone – had a large number of producers building commuter bikes. These included Adler, Ardie, DKW, Dürkopp, Express, Hercules, Maico, NSU, TWN (Triumph), and Zündapp. Many of these marques were industry pioneers.

Technically innovative, although not a sales success, was the unusual Imme (1948–51). Designed by Norbert Riedl, it featured a 98cc, two-stroke engine with a single horizontal cylinder. The engine assembly and rear wheel were suspended as a unit, pivoting below the seat, while the connecting frame also formed the exhaust system.

ITALY

Italian manufacturers built a large number of small-capacity, two-stroke motorcycles during the late 1940s and throughout the 1950s, together with massive quantities of scooters and mopeds. They came from the likes of Aermacchi, Benelli, Bianchi, Guazzoni, Morini, Moto Guzzi, and Parilla.

Unusually, given its well-known, classic four-stroke models, Guzzi produced the most successful of the commuter bikes. It began with the 65cc Guzzino, also known as the Motoleggera. This tiny machine appeared in 1946. It had the traditional Guzzi horizontal cylinder, but instead of the usual piston porting of most small, mass-produced two-strokes, it used a rotary valve, as did the Cardellino (65 and 73cc) and Zigolo (98 and 110cc), which were developed from the same basic design.

left The BSA Bantam was one of the most popular of all commuter bikes, being built in a variety of engine sizes from 1948 to 1971. This is one of the original 125cc D1 models.

facing page, top A typical Italian commuter bike, the MV Agusta 125TEL (Turismo E Lusso), which was built between 1949 and 1954. The final version, seen here, sported a duplex frame, telescopic front fork and swinging-arm rear suspension. The 123cc, two-stroke engine produced 5bhp at 4,800rpm.

above Built in Greet, Birmingham, the James Comet was one of the least expensive commuter bikes. Powered by a Villiers 98 cc engine with a two-speed gearbox, it offered budget-priced motorcycling during the late 1950s.

right The 1953 German Express M200 was a high-quality machine. Powered by an Ilo 197 cc, single-cylinder, two-stroke engine, it featured a tank-top toolbox, individual sprung saddles and plunger rear suspension.

ENCLOSURE

During the late 1950s and early 1960s, enclosure – concealing parts of a motorcycle behind decorative bodywork, as opposed to adding streamlining to improve performance – gained favour with many manufacturers.

MILLER-BALSAMO

Well before the fashion for enclosure took hold, the Italian Miller-Balsamo concern produced two such motorcycles. The first (a 200cc two-stroke) appeared just before World War II and had panelling around the engine, and one of the star exhibits of the 1946 Milan show was the Jupiter. This revolutionary model carried the practice further with full enclosure of engine and frame. Powered by a 246cc, overhead-valve, single-cylinder engine, it was also notable because of its hydraulically controlled rear suspension and pneumatic front fork. In addition, it had a gear indicator on the instrument console.

NORTON SILVERFISH

Next came the Norton Silverfish. Also known as the "Kneeler", this, like the Featherbed frame, was the work of Ulsterman

Rex McCandless. The Silverfish used enclosure to the full, together with streamlining. The alloy bodywork featured a nose-piece that extended from a point about hub level ahead of the front wheel to (at the top) just above the handlebars, in line with the steering axis, and (at the bottom) to the cylinder-base level. The nose was wide enough for the front wheel to turn within it. Behind the nose, separate shields extended rearward, being profiled to the rider's thighs and arms. The rider adopted a semi-prone position – his shins were horizontal and his feet braced against the footrests adjacent to the rear-wheel spindle. In other words, the rider knelt on the bike. The rear was enclosed in a streamlined tail-piece.

Although not a success in racing, the Silverfish did break the one-hour world speed record in November 1953, with an average speed of 215km/h (133.7mph).

AERMACCHI CHIMERA

Star of the 1956 Milan show, the Aermacchi 175 Chimera had evolved from a sketch of "the ultimate motorcycle" drawn by Count Mario Ravelli, a notable automobile stylist of the time.

facing page Norton works rider Ray Amm with the innovative Silverfish. Although not a success as a grand prix racer, its enclosed and streamlined bodywork allowed it to set a new one-hour world speed record in November 1953.

left An Ariel Leader brochure from the late 1950s, showing details of the machine's enclosed bodywork.

above Several firms offered rear enclosure on their machines. Triumph's design was commonly known as the "bathtub". This is a 1961 650cc Thunderbird.

below Royal Enfield's effort was the Airflow, which offered a combination of streamlining and rider protection.

The details were filled in by Alfredo Bianchi, Aermacchi's design chief. The Chimera had die-cast aluminium panels enclosing the engine and frame, and inspired similar styling in other machines.

BRITISH EFFORTS

There is no doubt that the British efforts of the late 1950s and early 1960s were strongly influenced by the Chimera. The first of these, the Ariel Leader, took the concept a stage farther, however, by providing complete rider protection and also pioneered the use of plastic components on motorcycles. Designed by Valentine Page, the Leader was a 250cc, two-stroke twin.

Triumph and Norton offered rear enclosure for their twins, while Velocette enclosed the bottom half of its 350 and 500cc singles. Royal Enfield favoured the streamlined approach for its Airflow models, but without the rear enclosure.

Subsequently, enclosure went out of fashion, and then made a return in the mid-1980s with the Ducati Paso and the Honda CBR600/1000 models.

THE CZECH INDUSTRY

With France, Belgium, and Germany, Czechoslovakia was one of the original pioneering nations of the motorcycle. The famous Laurin & Klement marque, founded while the country was still part of the Austro-Hungarian Empire, was a serious threat to the likes of the Paris-based Werner brothers and the Belgian Minerva company at the turn of the 20th century. In 1918, after World War I, Czechoslovakia became an independent republic.

The two most famous Czech motorcycle brands are CZ and Jawa, although there have been many other marques over the years – almost a hundred of them.

CZ

Ceska Zbroiouka (CZ) was formed in 1918 to manufacture armaments and didn't begin building motorcycles until 1932.

Although the company produced street bikes and road racers, its most famous series after World War II was a family of motocross machines. All were piston-port, single-cylinder, two-stroke models, with twin exhaust pipes at first, then with a single high pipe.

The twin-pipe bike made its first appearance at the 250cc World Motocross Championships in 1960, ridden by Vlastimil Valek, who finished ninth. In 1964, CZ began selling the twin-pipe to private owners under the code 968, followed a year later by the very similar 360cc 969 version. At first glance, the larger-engined machine appeared simply to be a bored-out 250, but this was not the case. The smaller engine had a bore and stroke of 70.0x64.0mm; the 360, 80.0x72.0mm.

In 1967, CZ introduced the single-high-pipe models in world motocross competition. The 968 was updated to

left Jawa entered speedway with its two-valve 500DT, which was based on an existing ESO design. Later, like the 898 model of the early 1980s, it was given four valves.

right Jawa celebrated 50 years of motorcycle manufacturing in 1979. Its first machine had been based on the German Wanderer.

below During World War II, Jawa engineers managed to design a brand-new 250cc model of advanced design under the noses of the occupying Germans. This emerged, post-war, as the Springer – due to its plunger rear suspension and telescopic front fork.

become the 980, which, like the 360, had an almost-square aluminium cylinder. The revised 360 became the 969.01 model. It won the 1967 500cc championship, repeating the feat in the following year, when it was joined as champion by the 250. Both machines were standard bikes, identical to those sold to private owners. Thus, CZs became known as "out-of-the-crate racers".

JAWA

Jawa was set up in 1929 and employed the British designer George Patchett as chief engineer between 1930 and 1939. During World War II, although the country was under German occupation, the company managed to prepare for the postwar era by designing an ultra-modern, unit-construction, 248cc, two-stroke single, with twin exhaust pipes, automatic clutch,

telescopic front fork, and plunger rear suspension. Known as the Springer, it was joined in 1948 by a 350 twin, having the same cycle parts. At the end of 1953, the Swinger 250 and 350cc models appeared, utilizing the same engines. The main difference was that they had swinging-arm rear suspension. These machines were so good that they continued in production, almost unchanged, until the early 1970s.

Jawa began speedway racing in the 1960s with the 500DT (Dirt Track). Subsequently, the overhead-valve, single-cylinder engine was replaced by an overhead-camshaft unit, originally with two valves, and later four. Other features included total-loss lubrication, dry multi-plate clutch, rigid (unsprung) frame, and telescopic front fork. By the end of the 1960s, Jawa had become the world's largest producer of dirt-track (speedway, long-track, and ice racing) bikes.

WERNER BROTHERS 17-18   BELGIAN EFFORTS 26-27
DIRT-BIKE SPORT 134-135

CAFÉ RACER CULTURE

The "Swinging Sixties" was a period when, for the first time, the young had money to burn. In Britain, motorcycle manufacturers gave them something to burn it on with the latest batch of high-performance bikes, such as the BSA Gold Star, Norton Dominator, Royal Enfield Constellation, and Triumph Bonneville.

Films such as *The Wild One* and *The Leather Boys*, together with the potent pop music phenomenon rock 'n' roll, led to a new breed of young motorcyclist and a new breed of motorcycle – the café racer – which looked and performed more like a competition machine than a road bike.

RACING INFLUENCE

What really helped set the café racer apart from the rest was the influence of British short-circuit racing, which prompted many riders to attempt to re-create on the street what the racers did on the track. Moreover, some manufacturers built clubman's racers (such as the BSA Gold Star), many of which found their way onto the public highway. These, together with suitably modified touring models, formed the era's "ton-up" fraternity – road bikes capable of 160 km/h (100 mph). Racing components such as lightweight alloy or glass-fibre fuel and oil tanks, clip-on handlebars, rear-set foot controls, and the like became the hallmarks of the café racer.

THE RIDERS

Like their bikes, the riders also stood out, in their leather jackets, jeans, leather flying boots, and "pudding basin" or "space" helmets. Often, they congregated at all-night transport cafés (hence the name) and coffee bars, sipping steaming cups of frothy espresso to the blare of rock 'n' roll from the inevitable brightly lit jukebox. To make life interesting, they devised the practice of death-defying "burn-ups" from one café to the next. Or groups would make high-speed trips out of town, to the coast, or to spectate at race meetings, for example.

A COTTAGE INDUSTRY

A vibrant cottage industry sprang up to supply café racer goodies for those who wanted to convert an existing bike or to build a "special" by combining parts from different machines – notably the legendary Triton (a Triumph engine in a Norton Featherbed frame). Ready-made specials, such as the Dunstall Dominator and Rickman Metisse, were also available.

Only the arrival of large-capacity Japanese motorcycles, spearheaded by the 1969 Honda CB750, finally brought the café racer era to an end. Although many of its young devotees were villified, in retrospect, it seems an innocent time – without the excesses of many modern youngsters.

facing page To many, the BSA Gold Star DBD34 Clubmans was the ultimate café racer. It was, and still is, a motorcycle icon. Even standing still, it looks a fearsome beast.

top The famous Ace Café in North London – typical of the all-night transport cafés of the 1960s and a magnet for young British bikers of the day.

above Royal Enfield was one of the few British motorcycle companies to embrace the cult of the café racer, as this 1965 brochure reveals.

right The five-speed Royal Enfield Continental GT of the mid-1960s. Features included factory fitted clip-ons, flyscreen, rev-counter, racing-style tank, and bright red paint job.

5   THE RISI

NG SUN

above Early Honda designs, such as this 1964 C95 150cc twin, were notable for their advanced specification, which often included such features as push-button starting.

left A 1956 Hurricane 350cc single. The cycle parts and styling were modelled on the British Triumph marque.

facing page A young Barry Sheene, seen with Suzuki GB sales director Maurice Knight, taking delivery of his new GT550 triple, circa 1974.

THE RISING SUN

Between 1945 and 1959, the Japanese created a vast motorcycle industry, which, as the 1960s dawned, was ready to take on the world. Led by Honda, the Japanese manufacturers made their international debut, more or less simultaneously, on the racing circuit and in the showroom.

When they first appeared in Europe and North America, Japanese racing bikes were only moderately successful. Similarly, the production models, although technically innovative and loaded with standard features that would have been considered extras on native machines, appeared somewhat strange to the Western eye.

Within a few short years, however, this situation had changed drastically. Not only was almost every class of grand prix racing dominated by the Japanese, but also the likes of Honda, Bridgestone, Suzuki, Hodaka, and Yamaha were well-respected names, enjoying the strongest dealer network in the industry, in Europe, and North America.

So what had caused such a major reversal of fortunes? To begin with, the Japanese had created a firm foundation within their domestic market, which, by the end of the 1950s, was one of the strongest and fastest growing in the world. Next, they had planned a properly funded export drive, which included a substantial racing budget. In addition, they had recruited the right people in the various countries they had targeted for their sales invasion. Never in the entire history of motorcycling had one nation achieved such dramatic inroads into worldwide markets in so little time, and with such determination and efficiency.

But this was no mere marketing exercise. There were sound reasons behind the Japanese success story. Without exception, Japanese motorcycles featured an all-round excellence that neither the European nor American bike builders could match. Their strong performance, good build quality, high level of technical refinement, and value for money combined to make a winning formula. They could only be faulted in roadholding and handling, deficiencies that

were mainly due to "pogo-like" rear suspension units and poor tyre compounds.

Disregarding Honda's C100 Super Cub commuter, the top-selling motorcycle of the first generation of Japanese exports was the 305 cc Honda CB77, known in the USA as the Super Hawk. Even though it was a sportster, it bristled with technical refinement – sophistication even. Included in its comprehensive specification were such features as a push-button starter, a comfortable dualseat, a combined speedometer and rev-counter, twin rear-view mirrors, large silencers, 12-volt electrics, a proper air filtration system, and comprehensive mudguarding.

EARLY DESIGN

Today's Japanese motorcycle is a product of vast manufacturing facilities, features cutting-edge technology, enjoys worldwide sales, and plays a major part in most forms of motorcycle sport. Its almost unchallenged dominance is strictly a recent phenomenon, however, since before World War II very few people outside Japan knew that motorcycles were manufactured there; fewer still had seen, let alone ridden, one.

THE ORIGINS OF AN INDUSTRY

The first machine that could be classified as a motorcycle was imported into Japan from Germany in 1899. It was a steam-powered device with a pair of large wheels shod with solid rubber tyres, and a pair of small outrigger wheels.

In 1908, Narazo Shimazu designed and built the first motorcycle engine in Japan, fitting it into an imported Triumph chassis. The first all-Japanese design was constructed by the Miyata company in 1913. It was powered by a two-stroke engine and sold under the Asahi (Sunrise) name.

By the mid-1920s, vast crowds were watching dirt-track and road racing events in Japan, and, in 1927, Kenza Tada became the first Japanese rider to race in the Isle of Man TT. Most hikes were imported, however, including Tada's British Velocette. This situation continued until the outbreak of war in 1941.

A NEW START

World War II changed everything, leaving Japan a shattered country, with most of its production facilities and cities in ruins. In a few short years, however, an economic and industrial miracle came from this scene of desolation.

First into production were Meguro, Miyata, and Rikuo, closely followed by Tohatsu, Pointer, Abe Star, Hosk, Olympus, and Showa. Some marques had quaint names, such as Pearl, Queen Bee, Jet, Pony, Hope Star, and Happy. Several, among them Hosk and Hurricane, clearly followed British designs, while Fuji and Honda leaned toward German technology.

By 1952, a peak of around 120 marques had been recorded, but few survived until the late 1950s. Those that did were headed by Honda, Suzuki, and Yamaha. Others included Meguro (later taken over by Kawasaki), Tohatsu, Pointer, Bridgestone, Lilac, Liner, and Rabbit.

RAPID GROWTH

Although there were fewer Japanese marques in production after the war, more bikes were manufactured. In 1945, for example, only 127 machines had been built, but by 1950 production had risen substantially to 2,633. Five years later, this figure had increased to 204,304. And by 1960, it had reached an amazing 1,349,000 motorcycles.

By this time, Japanese design had largely moved away from outside influences. This new-found independence coincided with grand prix racing campaigns, employing new multi-cylinder machines, and technical innovations such as push-button starting, direction indicators, improved electrics, and race-bred performance.

facing page The Sunyu 250 cc, overhead-camshaft single was typical of Japanese motorcycles of the late 1950s.

left Built around 1959, this Lilac MF39 had a narrow-angle V-twin engine, modelled very much on the German Victoria Bergmeister. It featured shaft drive.

below left The 1950s Hosk 500 cc, overhead-valve, vertical twin was similar in style to British designs of the period.

bottom left One of the early pioneers of the Japanese industry was Meguro, later taken over by Kawasaki. This is a typical Meguro 500 cc, overhead-valve model of the immediate postwar era.

THE HONDA MOTOR CO.

Soichiro Honda was born on 17 November 1906, the son of a blacksmith, in Komyo, long since swallowed up by the urban sprawl of modern-day Hamamatsu. From an early age, he showed an interest in anything mechanical, and at school displayed a distinct leaning toward practical matters.

HONDA'S EARLY CAREER

After leaving school in 1922, Honda served his apprenticeship as a car mechanic. In the early 1930s, he opened his own garage and did well enough to take up car racing. This ended abruptly, however, after a serious accident in 1936. He sold the business and began manufacturing piston rings.

At the outbreak of World War II, Honda developed a machine so that piston rings could be produced by unskilled women. Toward the end of the war, in early 1945, his factory was heavily bombed, and after the conflict he sold out to Toyota, taking a year off.

THE FIRST MOTORCYCLES

In October 1946, Honda set up the impressive-sounding Honda Technical Research Institute. In fact, it was little more than a wooden hut, on a levelled bomb site on the outskirts of Hamamatsu.

Postwar, the Japanese were in dire need of personal transport, provided it was cheap, and Honda had discovered a cache of 500 small engines (intended for military generators). By adapting these tiny power units and fitting them to conventional pedal cycles, he took his first step toward becoming the world's largest motorcycle manufacturer, which he achieved in little more than 15 years.

Soon he was overwhelmed with orders, and the stock of engines dwindled rapidly. So, to meet demand, he set out to design and build a petrol engine of his own. The result was the 49cc, two-stroke, single-cylinder Type A, which appeared in 1947. When the Honda Motor Company was incorporated in September 1948, the Type A had obtained a 60 percent share of the domestic market.

THE FIRST FOUR-STROKE

The Type E, introduced in mid-1951, was Honda's first four-stroke motorcycle. It featured an unusual three-valve arrangement (two inlet, one exhaust) and two carburettors. Although the newcomer set a new record for Japanese motorcycle production of 130 units per day, Honda was not without problems and, in 1953, he was almost forced out of business due to cash-flow problems, only to be saved by his bank.

Honda was a fighter, however, and a series of new designs helped the company progress throughout the 1950s.

SUPER CUB

The breakthrough came in 1958, with the debut of the C100 Super Cub commuter bike. Introduced in October that year, it sold in vast numbers – production in 1959, for example, reached an incredible 755,589 machines.

Until this time, the world's motorcycle makers had largely concentrated on enthusiast models, which effectively limited sales. The new 49cc (40.0x39.0mm bore and stroke), overhead-valve, "step-through" single gained Honda a vast new market from the man (and woman) in the street. By 1983, a staggering 15 million Super Cubs had been sold.

left A 1964 Honda C95 tourer, with overhead-camshaft, twin-cylinder engine, leading-link front fork, electric starter, full-width alloy hubs, direction indicators, and whitewall tyres.

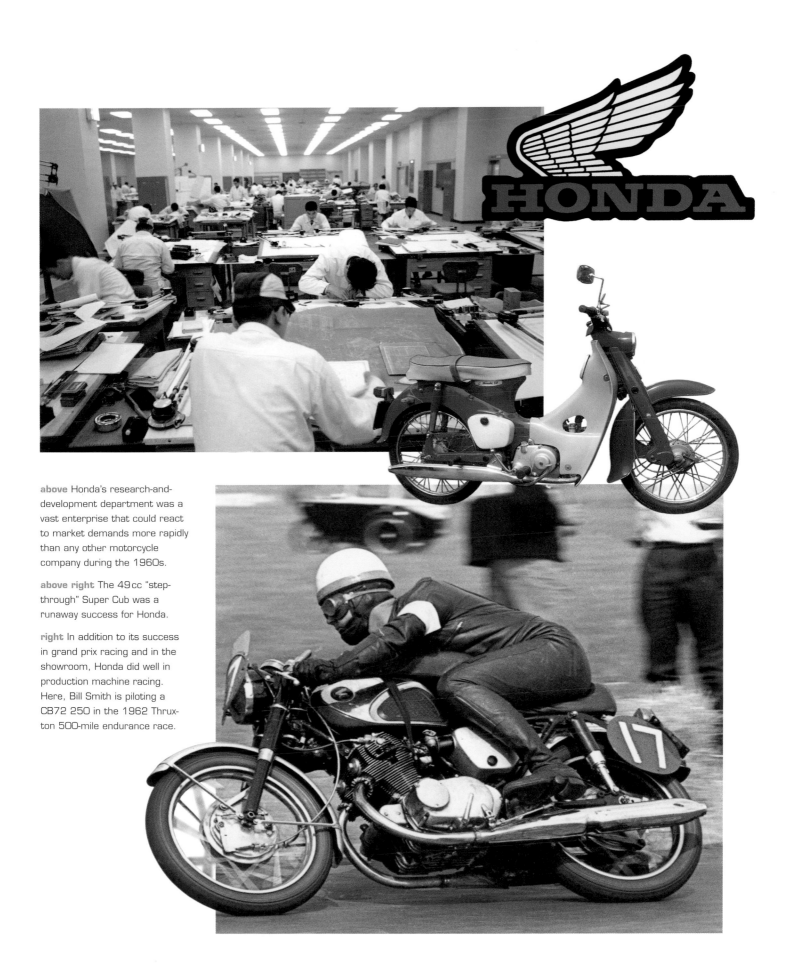

above Honda's research-and-development department was a vast enterprise that could react to market demands more rapidly than any other motorcycle company during the 1960s.

above right The 49cc "step-through" Super Cub was a runaway success for Honda.

right In addition to its success in grand prix racing and in the showroom, Honda did well in production machine racing. Here, Bill Smith is piloting a CB72 250 in the 1962 Thruxton 500-mile endurance race.

THE HONDA MOTOR CO.   **117**

above The 1968 Suzuki AS50 had the marque's Posi-Force lubrication system.

right Among the other advanced features of the Suzuki AS50 were rotary-valve induction and a five-speed gearbox.

LUBRICATION ADVANCES

Although advances in performance were exhibited by many Japanese designs, an important – and often overlooked – feature was the increased sophistication of the product. Nowhere was this more apparent than in two-stroke engine lubrication.

THE BACKGROUND

Four-stroke and two-stroke motorcycle engines of conventional design have entirely different lubrication systems. The former have pressure-fed crankshaft bearings, so inevitably a lot of oil is splashed around the crankcase. Such a system would be impractical in a normal two-stroke, where the crankcase serves as a primary compression chamber for the incoming petrol/air mixture. This would pick up so much excess oil mist that the exhaust would be excessively smoky and the spark plugs would be prone to fouling.

The two-stroke solution is to transfer a small quantity of oil into the crankcase with the mixture. For many decades, two-stroke motorcycle fuel tanks contained "petroil", an oily mixture

that was delivered by the carburettor to the crankcase. This primitive arrangement worked surprisingly well, but had the disadvantage of causing a smoky exhaust under light and heavy loads, and reducing lubrication when slowing or shutting the throttle.

THE METERED PUMP

The Japanese, notably Suzuki and Yamaha, pioneered the use of a separate oil tank, which fed a variable metering pump controlled by the throttle, in the modern high-performance two-stroke engine. This load-linked oiling concept was not a Japanese innovation, however – the Italian Adalberto Garelli and the British Velocette marque had already employed the principle. What the Japanese did was to refine the system and make it suitable for mass production.

The basis for the system is a pump driven by the engine, its output being proportional to engine speed. The output is controlled by an adjustable nozzle that is varied in area by a

To Oil Tank

To Throttle Grip

Sprayed to small end

Transmission oil

To gear box

above and right Details of the Posi-Force lubrication system.

below right A Yamaha YDS5 twin-cylinder engine, showing the oil tank for the machine's pumped lubrication system.

mechanism linked to the throttle control. This allows the maximum pump delivery to be achieved at full throttle, but progressively restricts output as the throttle is closed. The pump draws oil from the separate tank and delivers it under pressure to the crankshaft bearings and the cylinder walls, from where it reaches the big-ends and other bearing surfaces as a mist or by being thrown against them by centrifugal force.

ENVIRONMENTALLY FRIENDLY

Such an oil-injection system allows oil flow to be kept to the minimum, reducing consumption and pollution, yet allowing the engine's power to be turned on or off without adverse effects. There is no doubt that it has played a major role in ensuring that the two-stroke remains acceptable in the modern, environmentally conscious, world.

GRAND PRIX TECHNOLOGY

During the 1950s, Japanese manufacturers began to show an interest in world championship grand prix racing. Toward the end of the decade, they sent observers to European circuits to study and photograph the latest racing motorcycles.

HONDA STARTS THE BALL ROLLING

Then, in 1959, Honda arrived on the European racing scene with a squad of 125cc, double-overhead-camshaft twins. These were reliable, if not terribly fast, and they won the team prize in the Isle of Man TT.

The following year, Honda returned to Europe with a twin-cylinder 125 and a four-cylinder 250. The former had been modified in several ways since its TT debut, most of the changes affecting the chassis – it had a new frame and a telescopic front fork in place of the leading-link original. A lower centre of gravity and improved streamlining helped further. Although Honda did not win a title in 1960, it did gain ground on the European opposition.

In 1961, a strong Honda team overtook the Italians, the twin-cylinder 125 winning that year and in 1962 – with little modification. Meanwhile, Mike Hailwood took the 250 four to its first world championship in 1961, a feat that was repeated by Jim Redman the following season.

From then on, Honda continued to amaze, with a succession of new, high-tech racers, including a 350 four (1962), a 125 four (1965), a 50 twin (1965), a 125 five (1966), and a 500 four (1966). The opposition was crushed, however, by the 250 six, which appeared in late 1964, followed by a 297 version in 1966.

YAMAHA

Yamaha made its first appearance in European grand prix racing during 1961, with prototype 125 and 250cc models. Clearly derived from the MZ, these "guinea pigs" were being tested prior to a full-scale attempt at the world championships. This occurred in 1963 with the RD56 disc-valve twin. It was not until 1964, however, when Yamaha signed rider Phil Read, that it won the championship.

facing page Yamaha sold twin-cylinder racers that could win at the highest level. Mick Grant is seen here in 1973 with a liquid-cooled example.

right Tohatsu also sold machines with race-winning potential.

below Yamaha's 1966 full works GP RD05A 250cc four, with liquid cooling and eight speeds.

below right During the early 1960s, Honda's four-stroke four dominated the 250cc World Championship.

bottom right Phil Read won the 250cc World Championship for Yamaha in 1964 and 1965.

The arrival of the new Honda 250 six spurred Yamaha to design its 125 and 250cc, 90-degree V4s. After winning the 125 and 250 titles in 1968, Yamaha retired (Honda had quit at the end of 1967).

SUZUKI

Although Suzuki had contested the Isle of Man TT in 1960, it was not until the 1962 season that the marque really began to be competitive. Its increased success at that point was due in no small part to the defection of MZ rider Ernst Degner to the Suzuki camp. Degner and Suzuki became the inaugural 50cc champions in 1962, using the MZ-inspired, single-cylinder, disc-valve, two-stroke single. In addition to the Suzuki 50 (which was later built in twin-cylinder guise with liquid cooling and no fewer than 14 gears) and 125 twins, the company produced the RZ250. This model employed the square-four engine layout – but unlike the famous Ariel design, the Japanese machine was a disc-valve two-stroke with liquid cooling and a six-speed gearbox.

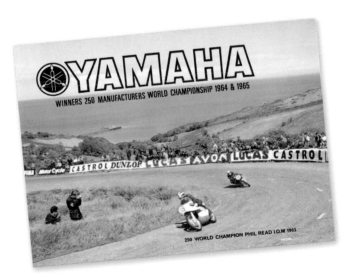

GRAND PRIX TECHNOLOGY

THE KAWASAKI TRIPLE

Of the Japanese "Big Four", Kawasaki was the last to begin manufacturing motorcycles. Unlike Honda, which had been established to build two-wheelers, Kawasaki was a substantial industrial concern already in heavy engineering, making trains, ships, and aircraft.

ENGINES FIRST

During the 1940s and 1950s, Kawasaki had been a major supplier of engines to the fledgling Japanese motorcycle industry. After co-operating with Meguro, it acquired the marque in 1963 and began building its own bikes.

A landmark in the evolution of the all-Kawasaki motorcycle occurred in September 1968 with the launch of the 499cc H1 Mach III (known in Japan as the 500-SS). This was an across-the-frame, three-cylinder two-stroke with piston-port induction (previously, the marque had employed disc valves on its 250 and 350cc twins).

Other features of the newcomer included a pressed-together crankshaft (allowing one-piece con-rods to be used), six main bearings (all ball races) and horizontally split crankcases. Four oil seals were fitted – two at the shaft ends and the remaining pair between the inner main bearings. The three cylinder barrels and heads were separate castings.

UNIT CONSTRUCTION

A five-speed gearbox and wet multi-plate clutch were built in unit with the engine. The lubrication system followed normal Kawasaki two-stroke practice, oil being injected by pump into the inlet tracts from an independent supply. The power output was 60bhp at 7,500rpm, and the machine was endowed with rocket-like acceleration.

A closely related racing version, known as the H1R, was developed by the end of 1969. In addition to a higher state of tune, it had a close-ratio gearbox and a dry clutch. It employed a supplementary "petroil" mixture to improve lubrication.

OTHER VARIANTS

After the original H1 street bike, Kawasaki introduced the H1A (1971), H1B (1972), H1D (1973), H1E (1974), H1F (1975), and, finally, the KH500 in 1976.

While the H1 was exciting, the H2 (Mach IV) was truly awesome. It had the same basic layout, but was equipped with a 748cc engine that produced 74bhp at 6,800rpm. Its performance, at least in a straight line, could not be matched by any other contemporary series-production roadster. This was offset somewhat by extremely high fuel consumption. The 750 H2 was built between 1971 and 1975.

Other Kawasaki triples included the S1 (249cc), S2 (346cc), and S3 (400cc). The S1 model became the KH250 in 1976, the S3 the KH400 in the same year.

The world fuel crisis of 1974 killed the design, however, Kawasaki being forced to explore new avenues in its quest to establish itself in the world market. The result was its series of double-overhead-camshaft, across-the-frame fours, beginning with the 903cc Z1 in 1972.

left Kawasaki works rider Mick Grant with his KR750 triple, circa 1976.

facing page:
top The original H1 (Mach III) arrived in time for the 1969 season and was developed over the following years. The KH500 model (shown) appeared in 1976.

bottom Kawasaki also produced smaller triples, like this KH250 and the KH400.

6 RACING IMPROVES THE BREED

above Mick Grant winning the 1974 Isle of Man Production TT on the famous Triumph Trident "Slippery Sam". This machine was victorious no fewer than five times between 1971 and 1975.

left The Italian Ducati marque built the limited-production 200 cc Motocross to special order in 1959 and 1960.

facing page Yorkshireman Denis Parkinson and the 499 cc, double-overhead-camshaft Manx Norton, with which he won the 1954 Manx Grand Prix.

RACING IMPROVES THE BREED

In 1949, the Fédération Internationale Motorcycliste (FIM) adopted the structure of an official racing series, leading to the first road racing grand prix world championships. That year, six circuits were used. Only the premier 500 cc solo championship was staged at all six of them, however; the 350 cc championship took place at five; the 250 cc at four; and the 125 cc and sidecars only at three.

In those early days, all the leading contenders employed four-stroke engines, normally with overhead camshafts (single or double) and one or two cylinders. In succeeding years, however, this pattern would change considerably.

The Italian Gilera four-cylinder racer won the 500 cc title in 1950, after the British AJS Porcupine twin had been victorious in 1949, but, surprisingly, a double-overhead-camshaft, single-cylinder Norton won in 1951 and 1952. This was due not only to Geoff Duke's brilliant riding, but also to Norton's excellent frame design. The work of Irishman Rex McCandless and nicknamed the "Featherbed", the frame out-handled anything else on the track.

Duke signed for Gilera for the 1953 season and, although his bike's frame was not an exact copy of the Norton's, the Italian four-cylinder machine benefited from a chassis that clearly showed British influence.

In 1950, the Gilera had been faster than the British bikes, but not until given a decent frame and Duke's unmatched riding skills did it become unbeatable. The

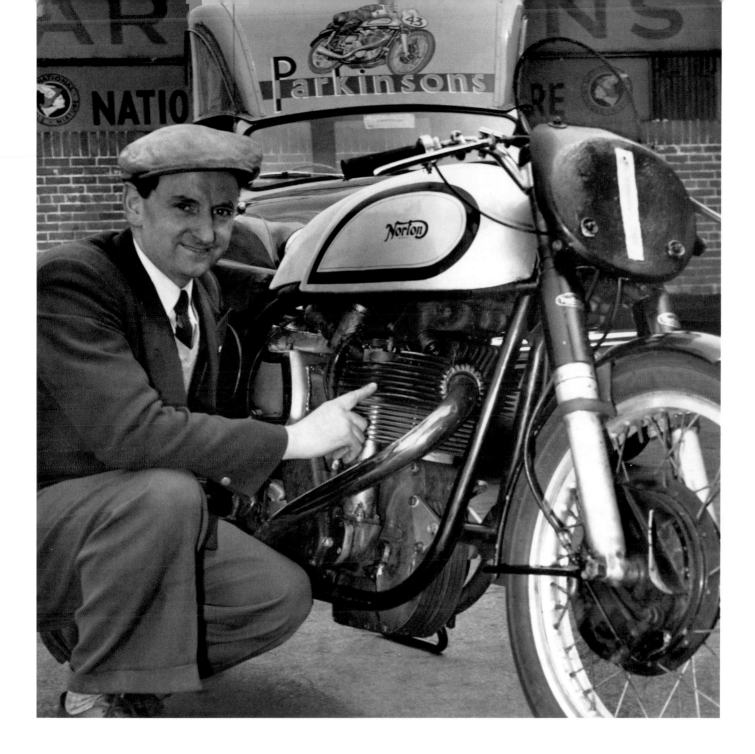

combination took a trio of world 500cc titles (1953, 1954, and 1955).

In 1956, another Englishman, John Surtees, won on an MV Agusta four, a feat he repeated in 1958, 1959, and 1960. The Italian Libero Liberati won in 1957 on the Gilera. In the smaller classes, the competition was even fiercer, with Italian MVs, Moto Guzzis, Gileras, FB-Mondials, and Ducatis taking on German BMWs, DKWs, and NSUs.

Although the British challenge faded in the grand prix classes, it made a return in Formula 750 (later Superbike), when such motorcycles as the BSA Rocket 3, Triumph Trident, and Norton Commando vied for honours.

The other major motorcycle sport was scrambling (later known as motocross). During the late 1940s and the 1950s, the premier 500cc class was dominated by heavyweight four-stroke singles. The 250cc mounts, however, were usually two-strokes. By the mid-1960s, overbored 250s, such as the 360cc CZ, Greeves, and Husqvarna, had challenged successfully for honours in the 500cc division. Only BSA, with its 441 and later 500cc, overhead-valve, unit-construction model (based on the existing C15 250cc design), managed to hold off the two-stroke hordes until, finally, CZ became champion in 1967.

Other forms of motorcycle sport included one-day trials, long-distance trials, speedway, grass-track, dirt-track, and ice racing.

left Norton built small batches of its Featherbed-framed Manx model between 1951 and 1962, and examples were raced all around the world. Here, Rudi Allison is shown leading the field in the 1952 South African Natal 100 – racing on dirt.

facing page:
top Rex McCandless' 1949 Norton Featherbed prototype.

bottom Percy May, 1971 British 500cc Champion, the last British champion on a British bike, with the exception of the rotary Norton. It was an amazing feat for what was, essentially, a 20-year-old design.

THE McCANDLESS FEATHERBED

By the end of the 1949 racing season, Norton's singles were facing opposition from Italian four-cylinder machines. To meet the threat and have any real chance of winning future world championships, it was clear to all concerned at the British company that drastic measures would be necessary.

REX McCANDLESS

The solution to Norton's problem was not destined to come from its own technicians, but from Belfast, Northern Ireland, where a young rider and engineer, Rex McCandless, had already created a superior form of motorcycle rear suspension. He had marketed conversion kits to allow this suspension to be fitted to existing rigid-framed machines, but subsequently had sold the business.

Freed from the pressures of running a business, McCandless set himself a new goal – to produce the ultimate racing chassis. A Norton engine was chosen for the project, which is not too surprising given that his great friend, Artie Bell, was a member of the Norton racing team.

McCandless could clearly see, however, that Norton's existing "Garden Gate" plunger frame (dating back to 1936) was well past its sell-by date.

A BRAND-NEW FRAME

Creating a brand-new racing frame was not an easy job and, working in great secrecy, McCandless produced several prototypes. All of them were tested by Bell.

Convinced that he was on the right track, he stuck to the

task. Then came the real breakthrough – he was offered a freelance position with Norton.

Surprisingly, Norton's first commission was not for a road racer, but a trials machine, the 500T overhead-valve single. After a truly awful 1949 season, however, McCandless was asked to design a racing frame for the company.

McCandless' frame was of duplex construction, the main portion comprising two continuous lengths of tubing. Each of these was attached to the base of the large-diameter steering head, from where they curved outward and ran horizontally to the saddle peak, dropped vertically, then ran forward to form the cradle for the engine and gearbox. Finally, they ran up and inward, passing between the top rails to be attached to the top of the steering head. The frame was braced at strategic

points by cross-tubes, while a large gusset on each side provided support for the rear engine plates, footrests, gearchange and brake pedals (the rear brake was cable operated on the racer), and the swinging-arm pivot fork. At the rear, the swinging arm was controlled by a pair of hydraulically damped shock absorbers.

Following track testing, rider Harold Daniell described the frame as a "featherbed", and the nickname stuck.

WORLDWIDE ACCLAIM
Geoff Duke went on to win three world championships with the Featherbed Norton, and the frame received worldwide acclaim in both its "wideline" and subsequent "slimline" forms. It set new standards in handling on the race track and the road.

TAGLIONI & THE DESMO

For almost 40 years, the Italian engineer and designer Fabio Taglioni was the inspirational force behind the extraordinary success of Ducati motorcycles on the road and the race track. His vision and talent for exploiting often radical ideas produced a series of motorcycles that established the company as the most charismatic of Italian sporting marques.

Born on 20 September 1920, Taglioni joined Ducati in the spring of 1954, following spells at Ceccato and FB-Mondial. His talent as a designer had been demonstrated by the V4 engine he had conceived while a student at Bologna university. It was not until his arrival at Ducati, however, that his talent was exploited to the full.

A DEBUT GP VICTORY

With the victory of Degli Antoni on a 125 cc Ducati in the 1956 Swedish Grand Prix, the Bologna-based company became one of the outstanding competitors at the top level of motorcycle racing. Antoni's death in a testing accident at Monza set back Taglioni's racing programme, but momentum

soon returned and, in 1959, a teenage Mike Hailwood won his first grand prix, the 125 cc Ulster, on a Ducati.

Both bikes ridden by Antoni and Hailwood had employed desmodromic ("desmo" for short) valve operation. The word "desmo" has long been associated with Ducati and Taglioni. In fact, many wrongly assume that Taglioni invented the system. Its theoretical advantages, however, have been known since the invention of the combustion engine itself. What Taglioni did was to make it work – on the track, and later in series-production roadster engines.

CONTROLLED RUN

"Desmodromic" was coined from the Greek words for "controlled run". The purpose of the design was to eliminate one of the chief problems of conventional sprung valve operation at high engine speeds, the phenomenon of valve float, or "bounce". This was a particular weakness at the time, before the advent of four-valves-per-cylinder technology and the rev limiters found in modern engine management systems.

facing page Englishman Tony Rutter won no fewer than four world TT F2 championships for Ducati during the early 1980s, riding the 600cc Pantah V-twin.

right Mike Hailwood gained many of his early victories aboard motorcycles designed by Fabio Taglioni, including his first grand prix – the 1959 125cc Ulster – on this machine.

below Fabio Taglioni at his drawing-board in the Ducati factory, Bologna.

below right Gianni Degli Antoni with the fully-streamlined, triple-camshaft 125cc Desmo single after winning the 1956 Swedish Grand Prix – the bike's first race.

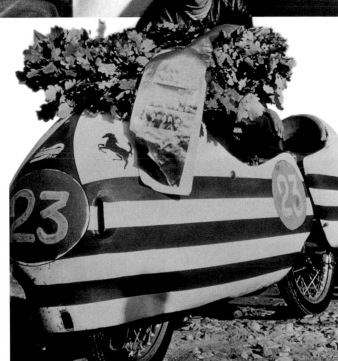

Valve bounce occurs when conventional valve springs are unable to respond fast enough to close the valves onto their seats. In a desmodromic system, the troublesome springs are replaced with a mechanical closing system, much like that employed to open them, thus providing a positive action. This effectively eliminates the bounce, allowing the engine to rev higher. Some desmo systems employ a separate camshaft (as in the 125cc Ducati Desmo single of the late 1950s) to close the valves, while others may simply have extra lobes on a single camshaft.

At first, the system was used exclusively on Ducati's racers, but subsequently the Italian company adopted it for series production with the introduction of the "wide-case" Mark 3D Desmo single in 1968. By 1980, all Ducati models featured desmodromic valve operation; a situation that continued into the 21st century.

DUCATI MACH 1 142-143   ITALIAN EXOTICA 156-157
DUCATI 202-203

TAGLIONI & THE DESMO

left Concentrating on the final speed test of the 1963 International Six Days Trial (left to right): Walter Winkler, Erich Bergauer, and MZ's design chief, Walter Kaaden.

facing page Ernst Degner astride his MZ 250cc, disc-valve twin prior to the start of the 1959 Ulster Grand Prix.

WALTER KAADEN

Generally known as the father of the modern two-stroke, Walter Kaaden was an engineering genius. Born on 1 September 1919, he gained his engineering diploma at the technical academy in Chemnitz. Later, he joined the Peenemunde research establishment, where the Germans developed their V-weapons during World War II.

Although Kaaden fell into American hands at the end of the war in 1945, they handed him over to the Russians. During the early 1950s, he was employed at the IFA factory at Zschopau. This had been the pre-war home of DKW, and from the mid-1950s was occupied by MZ.

DISC-VALVE INDUCTION

Walter Kaaden took charge of the MZ racing department in 1953, controlling all the marque's sporting activities. There, he developed a series of two-stroke engines, all of which had the carburettor mounted on the side of the crankcase, where it supplied the fuel mixture by means of a disc valve set in the crankcase wall. He was also a pioneer of the now widely used 54.0x54.0mm "square" bore and stroke dimensions (on a 125cc single), together with the expansion-chamber exhaust.

At the beginning of the 1953 season, the 125 had produced only 9bhp at 7,800rpm, but by the end of that year it was putting out 12bhp at more than 8,000rpm.

PORTING AND EXHAUST SYSTEMS

Much of the additional power that Kaaden had produced came from extensive changes to the transfer and exhaust ports, the compression ratio, and the exhaust system. In fact, Kaaden had made his most important breakthrough with the exhaust. He had been the first to recognize the importance of a highly resonant exhaust system (chamber). When combined with the extended port timing permitted by disc-valve induction, multiple transfer ports, and a squish-type combustion chamber, this gave huge increases in power compared with conventional piston-port induction.

By 1955, Kaaden had developed the disc-valve, two-stroke single to a point where it was almost on par with the very best of the previously all-conquering, twin-cam four-strokes. His work was largely ignored by the international community, however, as the Cold War was at its height, and East Germany was being treated like a leper.

A TWIN

Kaaden also designed and built a 250 two-stroke twin. His broad strategy was to experiment on the 125, then transfer the technology to the twin. In effect, the 250 was two 125s with their crankshafts spliced to a common primary drive. It was the first MZ to employ rearward-facing exhausts (from the cylinder barrels).

By 1961, the 125 single and 250 twins were offering the equivalent of 200bhp/litre, an amazing figure for the time, and MZ looked set to be world champion. Its top rider, Ernst Degner, defected to the West, however, and went to work for Suzuki. The Japanese manufacturer won its first world title in the following year.

DUCATI MACH 1

In the aviation world, "Mach 1" refers to the speed of sound. When testing a Ducati Mach 1 for the British journal *Motor Cycle News*, Pat Braithwaite wrote, "In a Lightning jet fighter, Mach 1 (plus a bit) takes you through the sound barrier. The new-for-1965 Ducati Mach 1 takes you through the ton barrier. And it's only a two-fifty."

ITALY V. JAPAN

Ducati's Mach 1 and Suzuki's Super Six were the fastest 250 cc street bikes of the 1960s, with a speed potential of 160 km/h (100mph). The Ducati introduced countless would-be racers to the sport, offering a performance that was not far short of genuine, over-the-counter racers, such as the Aermacchi Ala d'Oro and Bultaco TSS.

Ducati gained the advantage over Suzuki by putting the Mach 1 into production first. In Britain, it was introduced in September 1964, at the London Earls Court motorcycle show, where it caused a sensation.

CAREFULLY HONED AND DEVELOPED

The work of Fabio Taglioni, the Ducati Mach 1 was not a brand-new design; rather, it had been carefully honed and developed from the existing 250cc Diana (which had appeared in the spring of 1961). Both machines featured the Italian engineer's well-tried, overhead-camshaft, unit-construction, single-cylinder engine, with bevel drive to the camshaft and wet-sump lubrication.

The Mach 1 had a five-speed, close-ratio gearbox (the Diana had only four speeds), a three-ring, forged Borgo racing-type piston (with a 10.5:1 compression ratio), larger valves, a high-lift camshaft and a 29mm Dell'Orto SS1 29D racing carburettor with separate float chamber.

Other notable features included full-width, aluminium brake hubs, a frame that used the engine as a fully stressed member, rear-set foot controls, clip-on handlebars, a one-off curved kickstart lever, a racing-style seat (only on the original 1964 series – later Mach 1s had a conventional dualseat), and an eye-catching red and silver paint job. Among the optional extras, at additional cost, were a rev-counter and aluminium wheel rims.

A RACER FOR THE ROAD

In essence, the Mach 1 was very much a road racer – it performed, handled, and braked like a pure-bred grand prix bike. As practical, every-day transport, however, the Suzuki won hands down. With the T20 Super Six, the Japanese company had taken a giant step forward, offering such technical innovations as pumped lubrication and six speeds. The machine became the forerunner of a range of civilized, high-performance, Japanese twin-cylinder lightweights.

left Rider's view of the Mach 1. Note the optional Veglia racing rev-counter.

facing page:

top Classic-machine racer John Hynes winning on his Mach 1 at Brands Hatch, summer 1999.

bottom A 1964 brochure for Ducati's sensational Mach 1, the first series-production 250 capable of 160km/h (100mph).

PRODUCTION RACING

The racing of production motorcycles not only did much to sell the individual brands (especially if they won), but also helped develop the machines, particularly once factory participation began in the late 1950s. At the beginning of the 1970s, Formula 750 (later Superbike) racing evolved, challenging the established grand prix series. Yet another facet of production-bike competition was endurance racing. Subsequently, this and superbike racing achieved world championship status.

EARLY DAYS

Production racing began in the very early days of the motorcycle. For example, French Werners and Czech Laurin & Klements clashed in the 1902 Paris-Vienna event. This was a gruelling 990km (615-mile), four-day event, which involved scaling the Arlberg Pass, some 1,800m (6,000ft) above sea level, over largely unsurfaced roads.

As motorcycle development progressed, road racers fell into one of three categories: specialized grand prix (factory) racers, factory-built production bikes, and production (sports) machines. The last are considered here.

THE BOL D'OR

The beginnings of the legendary French Bol d'Or 24-hour race can be traced back to 1922 (when it lasted for 48 hours!). This first event was held at the Vaujours circuit. Since then, various venues have been used, including St Germain, Fontainebleau, Mont'lhéry, and, finally, Le Mans. It is the longest-running day-and-night event in the motorcycle racing calendar. During the 20th century, the most successful rider and motorcycle combination in Bol d'Or history was Gustave Lefevre and his Norton 500cc International. The pairing gained six victories between 1947 and 1957.

facing page A 600cc BMW R68 was used to win Australia's first 24-hour motorcycle race, at the Druitt circuit, New South Wales, in 1954.

above In the early 1970s, a production race was held during the annual international meeting at Silverstone. It featured a "Le Mans" start, where riders sprinted to their machines.

right The Norton Commando was popular for production racing. Note the high-level exhaust system.

THRUXTON

In Britain, Thruxton airfield, in Hampshire, was the scene of countless production racing battles during the 1950s–70s. The first event (lasting nine hours) took place in June 1955. By the beginning of the 1960s, the race had been set at 805km (500 miles) and had become a hotbed of competition between such marques as Triumph, BSA, BMW, and Norton. Each of the first three won races, but Norton was victorious three years running. By the beginning of the 1970s, the competitors were mounted on Norton Commandos, Honda CB750s, BSA Rocket 3s, and Triumph Tridents.

BARCELONA AND SPA

Other long-distance production races took place in Spain at Barcelona and in Belgium at Spa-Francorchamps. Kawasaki and Honda were the first Japanese manufacturers to realize

how vital these marathons could be to their development programmes. Eventually, Suzuki and Yamaha followed the same route, as did BMW, Ducati, and Laverda during the 1970s. Many of the components motorcyclists accept as standard equipment today were developed and tested in the heat of competition, including cast-alloy wheels, front and rear disc brakes, aerodynamic streamlining, multi-valve engines, twin headlamps (for maximum night vision), and aircraft-type, quick-action filler caps. Other race-inspired features are monoshock rear suspension, aluminium frames, inverted front forks, and exotic materials for producing strong and very lightweight engine components for increased performance.

There is no doubt that production racing, in all its forms, has greatly assisted motorcycle development. Moreover, because the machines are based on series-production bikes, the ordinary rider has benefited from that improvement.

7 SUPERBI

KES

below The 981cc, double-overhead-camshaft, three-cylinder Laverda Jota created history in 1976 by becoming the first series-production road bike to achieve 224km/h (140mph).

facing page Following Mike Hailwood's comeback victory on a 900cc Ducati V-twin in the 1978 Isle of Man TT, the Italian marque introduced the MHR (Mike Hailwood Replica) for 1979. It was Ducati's top-selling model during the early 1980s.

SUPERBIKES

In 1969, Honda introduced its ground-breaking four-cylinder, four-stroke CB750, and the age of the superbike had begun.

Although revolutionary for a series-production roadster, the across-the-frame engine configuration of the CB750 had been employed by the Italians, and Honda itself, to win grand prix races and world championship titles. Even so, given the general conservative nature of motorcyclists at the time, Honda had made a bold move. But it worked, reinforcing the Japanese company's position as world leader in the industry.

At first, Honda's Japanese rivals attempted to compete with high-performance two-strokes, among them the Kawasaki H1 Mach III, Suzuki GT750, and Yamaha YR3. It was not until the arrival of Kawasaki's 903cc, double-overhead-camshaft Z1

four in 1973, however, that the CB750 finally met its match. Producing 82bhp, the Z1 had a maximum speed of 210km/h (130mph). Like the CB750, it sported a disc front brake, electric starter, five-speed gearbox and full instrumentation.

By 1977, Kawasaki had increased the bike's capacity to 1,015cc, creating the Z1000. Like Honda, with its GL1000 GoldWing flat-four and CBX1000 six, however, this was not enough, and in 1978 the Z1300 arrived, with a liquid-cooled, across-the-frame, six-cylinder engine and shaft final drive.

The other Japanese marques were much slower to follow the four-stroke fashion. Suzuki launched its double-overhead-camshaft GS750 in 1977, while Yamaha's XS750 triple appeared a year later.

THE EUROPEAN RESPONSE

BMW's long-awaited replacement for its Earles-fork "boxer" twins was introduced at the Cologne motorcycle show in late 1969, in the shape of the Stroke 5 series, one of which was the R75 750. Then, in October 1973, the R90S 900 sportster arrived, followed by the fully faired R100RS 1000 in September 1975. All of these machines proved popular, although their high prices restricted sales.

During the 1970s, however, many motorcyclists looked to Italy for flair in styling and design, and they were not disappointed. Almost at the drop of a hat, the likes of Benelli, Ducati, Laverda, Moto Guzzi, and MV Agusta produced a glittering array of exotic superbikes.

Each of these marques was able to retain its identity with different engine configurations. Benelli chose the multi-cylinder route, with across-the-frame fours and sixes; Ducati, the 90-degree, inline V-twin; Laverda, parallel twins and across-the-frame threes; Moto Guzzi, 90-degree, transverse V-twins (with shaft final drive); and MV Agusta, a double-overhead-camshaft four based on its world championship-winning racing bikes.

Meanwhile, the British and American manufacturers continued to offer largely the types of machine that they had sold in the previous decade. Specialist producers, however, such as Dunstall, Rickman, and Bimota, found a niche market selling re-framed Japanese multis.

BMW R100RS

BMW's long-awaited replacement for its Earles-fork "boxer" twins series (introduced in 1955) made its first appearance at the Cologne motorcycle show in September 1969. There were three versions: the R50/5, R60/5, and the R75/5. The engine remained an overhead-valve, horizontally opposed twin (enlarged to 750cc) with shaft final drive, but there were many new features, such as an electric starter, flashing indicators, a five-speed gearbox, and a telescopic front fork.

THE R90S

In October 1973, BMW made its next move, with the R90S, dubbed "Germany's sexiest superbike" by the press. The choice of the Paris show for its debut was an obvious move, since at that event 50 years before, almost to the day, BMW had launched its very first bike, the R32.

In its styling – by Hans Muth – the R90S represented a milestone in the company's history. It featured a dual "racing" seat, a fairing cowl, twin hydraulic front disc brakes, and an exquisite, airbrushed, custom paint job for the bodywork, which ensured that no two machines looked the same.

ENTER THE R100RS

The Cologne show in September 1976 heralded the Stroke 7 series, which included a new concept for BMW (and the industry as a whole) – the fully faired R100RS.

A major feature of the R100RS was its comprehensive fairing. To achieve the optimum shape, BMW hired (at considerable cost) Pininfarina's wind-tunnel in Italy. The resulting streamlined bodywork not only added additional speed, but also provided the rider (and passenger) with a level of weather protection previously undreamed of by earlier generations. The 980cc (94.0x70.6mm bore and stroke) engine was the most powerful development of the two-valves-per-cylinder, pushrod flat-twin in a road-going machine, giving a genuine 70bhp. This and the comprehensive fairing gave a maximum speed approaching 208km/h (130mph).

THE FINEST SPORTS/TOURER EVER?

Many enthusiasts consider the original 1977 R100RS to be the finest sports/tourer ever built. There have been faster machines, even bikes that handled better, but none to match the all-round abilities of the R100RS. Another important feature was the 24-litre (5.25-imperial-gallon; 6.5-US-gallon) fuel tank, which provided a range of almost 480km (300 miles) if the bike was ridden gently.

The other models in the Stroke 7 series were the R100/7, the basic unfaired version; the R100S, successor to the R90S; the R100RT, with its "barn-door" fairing; and the R75/7 (later replaced by the R80/7).

The R100RS was dropped following the launch of the K Series, but was subsequently re-introduced in response to public demand. However, many people considered the re-issued bike an inferior machine because its power output was reduced to 60bhp.

left Introduced in 1976, the BMW R100RS featured a comprehensive fairing that had been developed in the wind-tunnel belonging to famous Italian coachbuilder Pininfarina.

facing page To many, the R100RS represents the ideal sports/touring motorcycle, with its excellent rider protection, powerful twin-cylinder engine, shaft final drive, and secure handling.

BMW R32 62-63   BMW K SERIES 178-179

1977 BMW R100RS SPECIFICATIONS

Engine Air-cooled, overhead-valve, transverse, flat-twin

Displacement 980cc

Bore and stroke 94.0 x 70.6mm

Ignition Coil, battery

Gearbox Five-speed, foot-change

Final drive Shaft

Frame All-steel, full duplex

Dry weight 210kg (462lb)

Maximum power 70bhp at 7,250rpm

Top speed 204km/h (127mph)

HARLEY-DAVIDSON

By the mid-1960s, Harley-Davidson was all that remained of a once great American motorcycle industry. Although it had entered into a transatlantic partnership with the Italian Aermacchi company in 1960, as far as large-displacement motorcycles were concerned, Harley-Davidson had stuck rigidly to its long-running, V-twin engine format.

In 1949, Harley-Davidson had introduced telescopic front forks. Then, in 1952, it switched to a foot gear-shift and a hand-operated clutch. The next big step came in 1958, with twin-shock rear suspension, celebrated by the company's top-of-the-range Duo-Glide.

THE ELECTRA GLIDE

In 1965, one of Harley-Davidson's most famous and revered models was introduced – the Electra Glide. This was the first of the company's bikes to be equipped with an electric, push-button starter, hence the "Electra" tag. The Harley marketing men called the Electra Glide "King of the Highway". And that's exactly how the rider felt, sitting astride all that glitter and excess. The "Glide" stood out in a crowd in the mid-1960s; later models continued to do that, even 40 years later.

A COMPETITOR

The Electra Glide cornered the market for such bold, luxurious, and expensive pieces of metal, at least until Honda introduced its GoldWing a decade later. Although the Harley and Honda appeared to be similar bikes, under the skin they were as different as chalk and cheese.

The GoldWing was a super-sophisticated, high-tech "Flash Gordon" to the Electra Glide's brash and up-front "Dolly Parton". Although far superior technically, the Japanese bike didn't have that magic name on the tank, which is what counted to many buyers.

As one journalist put it: "I don't know about you, but give me a piece of history to a piece of plastic any day!"

TECHNICAL DETAILS

When it first entered production, the Electra Glide had a 1,207 cc (87.0 x 100.0 mm bore and stroke) version of the familiar air-cooled, overhead-valve, V-twin engine, with a four-speed, foot-change gearbox. It remained that way until the arrival of the EVO (Evolution) engine in 1983. In Harley speak, it was as big an advance over the preceding Shovelhead as the Shovelhead had been over the Panhead.

Essentially, the new V-twin was an alloy-barrelled version of the Shovelhead engine, with a lighter valve-train and better breathing. It was also considerably lighter than the previous "iron" engine and produced more power. At the same time, the capacity was increased to 1,340 cc (87.3 x 100.8 mm bore and stroke), but it was still air cooled.

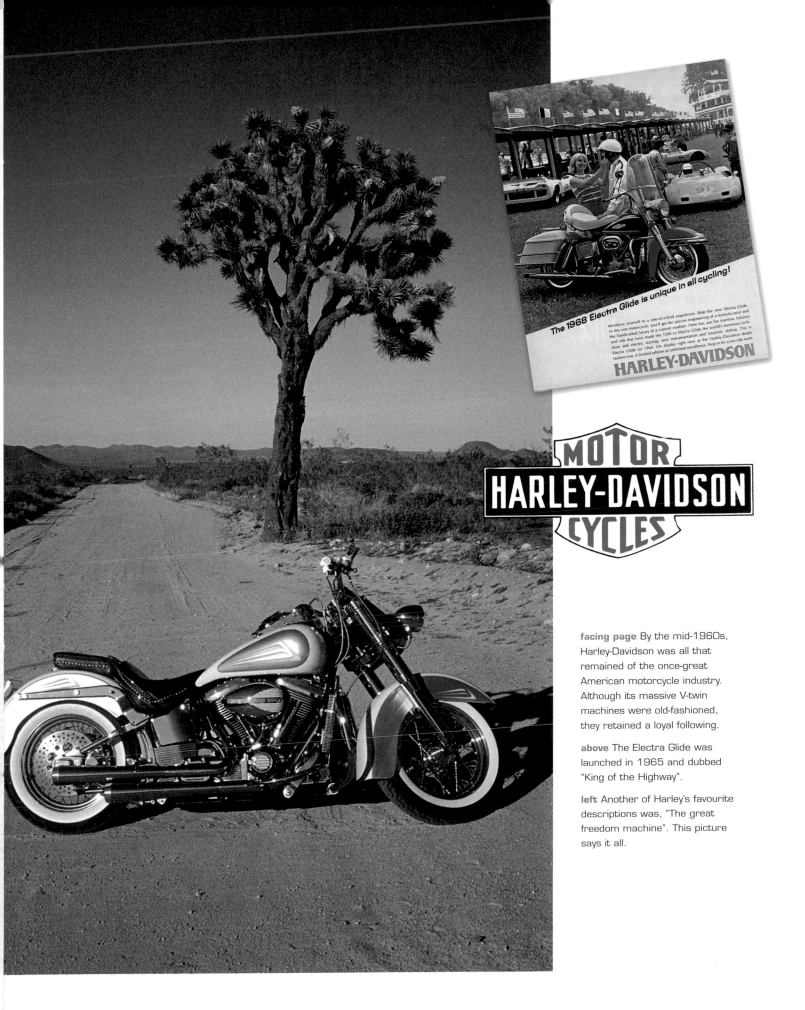

The 1968 Electra Glide is unique in all cycling!

Introduce yourself to a one-of-a-kind experience. Ride the new Electra Glide. In this one motorcycle, you'll get the precise engineering of a formula racer and the handcrafted luxury of a custom roadster. Here too, are the stamina, balance and ride that have made the 1200 cc Electra Glide the world's foremost cycle. Now add electric starting, new instrumentation and futuristic styling. This is Electra Glide for 1968. On display right now at the Harley-Davidson dealer nearest you. A limited edition of unlimited excellence. Stop in for a test ride soon.

HARLEY-DAVIDSON

MOTOR HARLEY-DAVIDSON CYCLES

facing page By the mid-1960s, Harley-Davidson was all that remained of the once-great American motorcycle industry. Although its massive V-twin machines were old-fashioned, they retained a loyal following.

above The Electra Glide was launched in 1965 and dubbed "King of the Highway".

left Another of Harley's favourite descriptions was, "The great freedom machine". This picture says it all.

8 THE MOD
MOTO

ERN
RCYCLE

THE MODERN MOTORCYCLE

During the 1980s and early 1990s, the world's motorcycle industry made great technical advances. For once, Honda didn't lead; instead, the front-runners were Japan's Kawasaki and Suzuki, Italy's Ducati, and Germany's BMW.

Although Honda continued to sell the most machines in the early 1980s, it seemed to lack a coherent strategy, at least in the big-bike field. This was typified by the company's series of V4 designs, which took much longer to develop than it anticipated. The other Japanese marques were left to push the boundaries of technology.

Kawasaki was the first to put a new generation of big-bore sports bikes onto the market, in the shape of the all-new GPZ900R (Ninja in North America). Shown to the press in December 1983, it was the world's first liquid-cooled, 16-valve, across-the-frame, four-cylinder production bike. The GPZ900R was also the first to employ a lightweight, diamond frame, aluminium sub-frame, and 406mm (16in) front wheel. Another feature was Kawasaki's innovative Uni-Trak monoshock rear suspension.

Suzuki really set things alight with its "racer-for-the-road" GSX-R750 of 1985. As the *American Motor Cyclist* magazine commented in its March 1996 issue: "Contemporary sports bike history is clearly divisible into two chunks: the Dark Ages, i.e. before the 1985 GSX-R750, and the Renaissance thereafter!" It wasn't simply that the GSX-R750 was the fastest; it was a complete sports bike, with superb performance, handling, and braking wrapped in a mouth-watering package.

facing page Kawasaki's ZX-10 arrived in late 1987, replacing the GPZ1000RX. With more power and torque, and a higher speed (272 km/h; 169 mph), it assumed the mantle of world's fastest production roadster.

below The Honda CBR1000F was built between 1987 and 1999. It began life as a sports bike, but was really a comfortable sports/tourer.

Of the European manufacturers, only BMW built anything that was really new in the first half of the 1980s, when it launched its K Series range. The first of these was the four-cylinder K100, soon nicknamed the "flying brick" because of the engine shape. From this, the K100RS sports/tourer and three-cylinder 750 K75 were developed. Later still came the 16-valve K1. All the K Series machines had fuel injection, which was an industry first. BMW was also the first to offer ABS (anti-lock braking) on a production bike, albeit originally as a cost option.

Ducati was taken over by Cagiva in 1985, and the marque introduced a number of innovative designs over the following decade, many penned by Massimo Tamburini. Engine development was carried out by Massimo Bordi, who had replaced Fabio Taglioni. The first to appear was the 750 Paso, in late 1985, but the really big news came two years later with the 851. This design was the first Ducati to incorporate four valves per cylinder, double overhead camshafts and fuel injection in the marque's 90-degree V-twin. Later, the 851 became the 888, with which Ducati won the first of many World Superbike titles in 1990.

In the superbike stakes, the first half of the 1990s was dominated by the Honda CBR 900RR FireBlade and Ducati 916. Other important developments that occurred during this time included the new 600 cc super sport class; improvements in handling, comfort, tyres, and braking performance; and the prevalence of digitally controlled ignition and fuel injection systems.

KAWASAKI GPZ900R

Launched in December 1983, the Kawasaki GPZ900R was a trend setter. Sold as the Ninja in North America, it had a liquid-cooled, 16-valve, double-overhead-camshaft, across-the-frame, four-cylinder engine. Other unique features were a lightweight, diamond main frame with aluminium rear section and 406 mm (16 in) front wheel. Kawasaki claimed that it was the first bike to have a front fork that delivered truly progressive wheel travel. At the rear was the company's rising-rate Uni-Trak suspension.

THE ENGINE

As with the earlier air-cooled Z1, the centrepiece of the new machine was its engine. To create a second-generation superbike, Kawasaki had carried out extensive tests on several configurations, including a V4, a V6, and an across-the-frame six, but none was found to offer any significant advantage over an across-the-frame four. Consequently, the proven layout was retained, although virtually every other aspect of the power unit was re-evaluated. The result was an all-new engine, which allowed Kawasaki – and ultimately the rest of the Japanese motorcycle industry – to take a giant step forward.

An important aspect of the 900R's engine was its compact size – it was narrower and less tall than that of the Z1. A major factor determining its smaller dimensions was a basic change in its layout. Liquid cooling meant that the cam chain could be positioned outside the cylinder bank, instead of in the centre. As a result, the wet-cylinder cooling system was both compact and highly efficient. Revving to 10,500 rpm, the one-piece crankshaft was supported by five plain bearings. In addition to driving the clutch, the crankshaft also drove a compact counter-balancer, which virtually eliminated secondary vibration. The clutch was operated hydraulically, while the gearbox contained six speeds – a first on a large-capacity Kawasaki motorcycle.

facing page The Kawasaki GPZ900R was a trend setter, being the first superbike with a liquid-cooled, 16-valve, across-the-frame, four cylinder engine.

above When launched in 1983, the GPZ900R was considered a sportster. Later, however, it became very much a sports/tourer and was often equipped with hard luggage.

right The high-tech, 114 bhp GPZ900R power unit was also used in a number of specials, including this show-winning, Harris-framed machine.

THE CHASSIS

A new, high-tensile steel frame reduced weight by about 5 kg (11 lb), compared with previous Kawasaki fours; it also lowered the centre of gravity. In the early stages of testing, standard downtubes were added to determine what stress, if any, they would counter. Results showed that the downtubes carried virtually no load, however, and they were discarded. A box-section, aluminium, rear swinging arm employed eccentric snail-cam chain adjusters.

Other features of the 900R included triple disc brakes, an anti-dive front fork, six-spoke alloy wheels, V-rated tyres, and a dry weight of 228 kg (503 lb).

Motor Cycle News recorded 254 km/h (158 mph) with the GPZ900R, while a trio of the bikes took the first three places at the 1984 Isle of Man TT. Technology moves on, however, and by 1985, the Kawasaki had been outstripped by even faster bikes, but it had been the first of the new breed.

KAWASAKI GPZ900R SPECIFICATIONS

Engine Liquid-cooled, double-overhead-camshaft, 16-valve, across-the-frame, four-cylinder

Displacement 908 cc

Bore and stroke 72.5x55.0 mm

Ignition Electronic

Gearbox Six-speed, foot-change

Final drive Chain

Frame Steel backbone, aluminium sub-frame and swinging arm

Dry weight 228 kg (503 lb)

Maximum power 114 bhp at 10,500 rpm

Top speed 254 km/h (158 mph)

ENDURO STYLE

The famous Paris-Dakar Rally, first staged for motorcycles in 1979, and the International Six Days Enduro (ISDE) – the latter replacing the long-running International Six Days Trial (ISDT) – were largely instrumental in the rise in popularity of enduro-styled bikes. These have been based on the successful works machines created by the likes of BMW, Cagiva, Gilera, Yamaha, and Honda.

PARIS-DAKAR

The first Paris-Dakar event, billed as "The World's Toughest Race", was won by Cyril Neveu on a modified Yamaha XT500 trail bike. However, BMW was the first manufacturer to really exploit the incredible 9,975km (6,200-mile) marathon, from the French capital to Dakar in Senegal, West Africa.

Competitors in the Paris-Dakar are faced with two weeks of biking torture, as first they meet the challenges of the Atlas Mountains and then the Sahara desert, one of the most inhospitable and dangerous places on Earth. Daytime temperatures soar well above 38°C (100°F), but it can freeze at night; sandstorms can blow up out of nowhere, scouring the face and obliterating the trail. The Paris-Dakar is truly the ultimate test of both man and machine.

THE BMW EFFORT

Special versions of the BMW flat-twin were victorious in 1981 and in 1983–85. After this record of four wins, BMW suffered a poor result in the 1986 event and subsequently announced its retirement from the rally (although it did return in the late 1990s).

Herbert Auriol is the only man to have won Paris-Dakar on two and four wheels. A former French trials champion, he won in 1981 on a BMW GS800, and in 1983 on a BMW 980. (In 1992, he was victorious in the car section, with a Mitsubishi.) Former World Motocross Champion Gaston Rahier, from Belgium, won the 1984 and 1985 events on 1,000cc BMWs.

All the German machines featured long-travel suspension, two-into-one exhaust systems and single, side-mounted rear shocks. BMW, together with Yamaha, pioneered the use of massive fuel tanks to allow over 580km (360 miles) to be covered without refuelling.

CAGIVA, YAMAHA, AND GILERA

After BMW quit, the main competitors were Cagiva, Yamaha, and Gilera. Cagiva used specially prepared, 900cc, Ducati-engined V-twins; the others used high-tech singles. The Yamaha 660 had five valves, six speeds, a long-travel front fork, and monoshock rear suspension. Gilera's RC600, which dominated its class in the early 1990s, displaced 558cc (98.0 x 74.0mm bore and stroke) and had a four-valve head, twin exhaust ports, a five-speed gearbox, and two TK carburettors.

HONDA EXP-2

Among the most technically interesting bikes ever used in the Paris-Dakar, however, are a pair of experimental 400cc Honda EXP-2 singles, which were entered in 1995. These employed active radial combustion (ARC) – a chemical self-ignition system that was related to the combustion process of the World War II German V2 rocket!

left BMW built enduro versions of its flat-twin for the Paris-Dakar Rally. These were victorious in 1981, 1983, 1984, and 1985.

facing page.
top A 1977 Ducati 125 Six Days enduro bike being put through its paces. The rear shocks could be mounted at an angle (as shown) or vertically.

bottom left The 2005 Husqvarna 610 featured monoshock rear suspension, an inverted front fork, and aluminium rear swinging arm.

bottom right During the late 1980s and early 1990s, Gilera won the 600cc class of the Paris-Dakar more than once with the liquid-cooled RC600R single.

BMW K SERIES

During the late 1970s, BMW's motorcycle sales were slipping, particularly in the USA. With warehouses full of unsold bikes, the chairman, chief engineer, and sales director all left the German company. Fortunately, their replacements, who joined in 1979, had considerable motor cycle experience.

THE SEARCH FOR A NEW IMAGE
BMW motorcycles needed a new image that encompassed more than the long-running flat-twin. In fact, one of the company's employees, Josef Fritzenwenger, was already looking for a replacement for the venerable model – something he had been doing since the mid-1970s, with little support.

Fritzenwenger's first idea was a water-cooled flat-four, but Honda's introduction of the same layout for its new GoldWing killed this off. BMW didn't want to appear to have copied one of its competitors.

COMPACT DRIVE SYSTEM
Eventually, Fritzenwenger came up with the concept of the compact drive system (CDS), after carrying out tests on a liquid-cooled, four-cylinder engine from a Peugeot 104 car. Originally, the aluminium engine had been inclined and mounted transversely in the 104. It occurred to the BMW engineer, however, that if he laid it flat, with its crankshaft in line with the frame, it could be just what he needed.

The configuration was ideal for shaft final drive, had a low centre of gravity, and offered good accessibility. Moreover, no other bike maker built a longitudinal and horizontal inline four – or had ever done so.

THE PROTOTYPES
Various prototypes – some with three cylinders, others with four – were built, ranging from 800 to 1,300cc. Ultimately, however, two engine sizes were selected for production: the 740cc K75 and 987cc K100. Both had 67.0x70.0mm bore and stroke dimensions.

Work began on the range in May 1979. The development team, now led by Stefan Pachernagg, concentrated initially on the four, which, as the unfaired K100, appeared in October 1983. This was followed by the far more popular K100RS facing page Dubbed the "Flying Brick" by many, the K100 employed BMW's compact drive system.

left In addition to bold styling, the K1 Super Sports model, which appeared in late 1988, was notable for having four valves per cylinder (a first for BMW's motorcycle division).

above Members of BMW's development team with their handiwork in September 1983, just prior to the launch of the K100.

sports/tourer and, finally, the LT version, which was equipped with a massive fairing.

A major innovation on the K Series BMWs was the use of Bosch LE-Jetronic fuel injection. Digital ignition was another significant advance.

THREE CYLINDERS

The three-cylinder K75 was launched in September 1985, the "S" version following in June 1986. Technically, the only major difference between the three- and four-cylinder models was the K75's contra-rotating balance shaft, which virtually eliminated vibration (a problem on the larger engine). It also had a modified R80 clutch and straight-cut gears.

The 16-valve K1 (with the K100's 987cc displacement) arrived in September 1988, further developments leading to 1,100 and 1,200cc models. In 2005, the brand-new 1,157cc, 163bhp K1200R (Roadster) and K1200S (Sport), with across-the-frame engines, were introduced.

1984 BMW K100 SPECIFICATIONS

Engine Liquid-cooled, double-overhead-camshaft, inline, flat-four

Displacement 987cc

Bore and stroke 67.0×70.0mm

Ignition Digital, integrated with electronic fuel injection

Gearbox Five-speed, foot-change

Final drive Shaft

Frame ubular space-type, engine used as stressed member

Dry weight 230kg (507lb)

Maximum power 90bhp at 8,000rpm

Top speed 215km/h (134mph)

SUZUKI GSX-R750

From the beginning, the GSX-R750 had been intended as a racer first, a street bike second. Its designer, Tansunobu Fujji, ensured that it met that criterion.

OIL COOLING

Initially, a working prototype of the machine was campaigned in endurance racing events during the early 1980s. One feature of this that was adopted for the production model, and which set the GSX-R apart, was oil cooling. Although this idea was not new, having been employed to help control the temperature of aero engines since the 1920s, it is important to understand the reasoning behind its use in a motorcycle.

Suzuki had opted for oil cooling to cure overheating problems encountered during development of its XN85 Turbo. Oil jets directed at the undersides of the pistons prevented the turbocharged engine from dropping molten metal into the crankcase. The same idea was used on the 1983 GSX-750EF sports/tourer to prevent the two central pistons from running hotter than the outer pair.

THE "R" ENGINE

While it would be accurate to describe the GSX motor as being air cooled with oil assistance, the emphasis was reversed on the "R" unit. Oil cooling came into its own in the new engine, which employed a second oil pump purely to remove engine heat. The primary pump, mounted on the same shaft and sharing a common housing, handled lubrication. A large oil cooler was mounted on the front frame tubes.

In answer to the question why Suzuki hadn't gone for water cooling, Fujji explained that it was because the air/oil-cooled engine was both narrower and lighter. A prototype liquid-cooled engine had proved this. Suzuki's attention to weight saving was a key aspect of the GSX-R and future "racer replica" designs.

AN ALUMINIUM CHASSIS

The "lowest weight" concept also led Fujji to create an aluminium chassis, both frame and rear swinging arm being constructed of this light metal. At the time, Suzuki claimed an

GSX R 750

facing page When the GSX-R750 arrived in 1985, it represented a significant advance in sports-bike technology, with its combination of performance, racer-like handling, and powerful brakes.

left The original air/oil-cooled GSX-R engine. Note the large aluminium oil cooler.

above Four-valve layout with Suzuki's twin-swirl combustion chamber (TSCC) design.

industry first, but it was wrong – the German Ardie marque had built roadsters with alloy frames in the early 1930s. The rear suspension itself was of the monoshock variety with a vertically mounted, rising-rate shock absorber.

The exhaust was another area where weight-saving techniques were applied. The GSX-R had a four-into-one system, rather than the heavier four-into-two arrangement or four separate pipes previously favoured by other marques.

The original 1985 GSX-R750 was an uncompromising sportster, being more at home on the track than city streets. As such, it was without equal in its day. A larger-engined version, the GSX-R1100, arrived to complement, but not replace, it in 1987.

1985 SUZUKI GSX-R750F
SPECIFICATIONS

Engine Liquid-cooled, double-overhead-camshaft, 16-valve, across-the-frame, four-cylinder

Displacement 749cc

Bore and stroke 70.0x48.7mm

Ignition Electronic

Gearbox Six-speed, foot-change

Final drive Chain

Frame Aluminium, Deltabox

Dry weight 176.4kg (388lb)

Maximum power 104.5bhp   10,500rpm

Top speed 249km/h (155mph)

SUPER SPORT

From the late 1980s, the most popular motorcycle category has been Super Sport, which refers to 600cc, multi-cylinder machines and, to a much lesser extent, 750cc twins. These bikes combine performance aplenty with relatively low weight and lower price tags than superbikes. The class has also become popular in racing.

KAWASAKI GPZ600R

After the huge success of its GPZ900R, Kawasaki realized that it had a winning formula. It also concluded that a scaled-down, more affordable machine could, potentially, be a top seller. The result was the GPZ600R of 1985, with which the Japanese marque stole a march on the opposition and created a brand-new sector in the market – 600 Super Sport.

A landmark in modern biking history, the 600R shared many design features with its larger and older sibling, such as liquid cooling, double overhead camshafts, an across-the-frame, four-cylinder layout, and four valves per cylinder. It was far from being simply a scaled-down GPZ900R, however, since the engine, while possessing many similarities to the 900R, was actually more closely related to the contemporary air-cooled GPZ550. The 592 cc (60.0 x 52.4 mm bore and stroke) unit duplicated the 550's central cam chain and chain primary drive with intermediate shaft and crank-mounted alternator, but was more compact, being 40 mm (1.6 in) narrower.

During its first two years, the GPZ600R had the field to itself. Kawasaki's Japanese rivals struggled to compete with old-technology, air-cooled bikes.

THE OPPOSITION FIGHTS BACK

By late 1986, Yamaha was able to announce the new FZ600 (albeit still an air-cooled design), and Suzuki was working on its own 600 sportster. Honda, meanwhile, was about to drop a big spanner in the works by announcing its brand-new, liquid-cooled, 16-valve CBR600F. This went on sale in early 1987, to great press and public acclaim, and it has remained a top seller into the 21st century.

HONDA CBR600F

The CBR600F's huge success was due to Honda's ability to keep it competitive, a series of updates over the years adding to the original's great all-round abilities. Even for a company the size of Honda, the CBR's success was phenomenal.

The original CBR had fully enclosed bodywork and a steel frame. Besides the almost yearly changes to power output, the first major revision occurred for 1991 and included a new exhaust, restyled bodywork and a modified frame. By 1995, the power output had grown to 100 bhp. Then, for 1999, there was virtually a new bike – including the engine – with, for the first time, an aluminium frame. In 2001, fuel injection replaced the original carburettors and power output was increased to 109 bhp at 12,500 rpm; in addition to the "F", a new sport model was available.

left Honda's CBR600 has been a best-seller in the middleweight super sport sector. The original CBR of 1987 had fully-enclosed bodywork and a steel frame.

above The Kawasaki GPZ600R of 1985 created a brand-new motorcycle category, the 600 Super Sport.

right In 1989, Yamaha launched the FZR600, which replaced its air-cooled FZ600. The new bike followed the company's "Genesis Concept" of inclined engine and Deltabox frame.

TOURING BIKES

For many years, touring bikes were big, heavy motorcycles with poor performance, dull handling, and less-than-perfect brakes. Modern machines, however, are entirely different.

HOW THE BREED EVOLVED

In the past, touring bikes were usually adapted from standard models, often with the addition of a sidecar. There were a few exceptions to this rule, such as Vincent's short-lived Black Knight of the mid-1950s and BMW's R60/R69S of the 1960s, but these were too expensive for most during the prolonged austere period that followed World War II.

With the arrival of the 1970s, the era of the modern superbike began, spurred on by the introduction of Honda's ground-breaking CB750 in 1969. The plethora of high-performance models that followed led to a demand for speed, but coupled to designs that could carry two people over long distances in comfort. BMW's R100RS and Moto Guzzi's SP1000 were the first of this new breed.

Today, most people in the developed world enjoy large amounts of leisure time, and for many, there is no better way to use that time than touring on two wheels. Motorcycle manufacturers have been only too eager to provide the means – in addition to the big four Japanese marques, BMW, Ducati, Triumph, Moto Guzzi, and Aprilia have all offered serious touring machines.

HONDA PAN EUROPEAN

One of the best Japanese designs has been the Honda Pan European ST. This machine is an excellent example of how to design and build the ultimate touring bike. Honda's engineering team began with a brief to create a fast, practical, and reliable mount, which it accomplished in superb fashion. The liquid-cooled V4 engine is superb, offering high torque and usable power in a smooth, unstressed fashion. This, coupled to excellent handling, powerful brakes, shaft final drive, and optional traction control system (TCS) and ABS, makes the ST one of the world's safest bikes.

BMW'S TOURING CHALLENGE

The German BMW company has always produced excellent touring models, and by the early 21st century it was the main competitor of the Japanese, with both twin- and four-cylinder models. BMW's K1200LT four-cylinder tourer was launched at the 1998 Munich motorcycle show. This giant among bikes challenged Honda's GoldWing in the heavyweight stakes at 378 kg (834 lb). Its 1,171 cc engine featured liquid cooling, double overhead camshafts, 16 valves, Bosch electronic ignition, and a six-speed gearbox.

Many, however, continued to opt for the R1100RT twin, launched in 1996, which is considerably lighter, but still boasts decent performance and a high-quality specification.

facing page With its liquid-cooled V4 engine, adjustable screen height and optional traction control, Honda's Pan European was much admired.

right The Moto Guzzi California FF 949cc, overhead-valve V-twin was offered with the choice of conventional carburettors or a fuel injection system.

below A luxury tourer: the 2006 Yamaha FJR1300A, with comprehensive weather protection and excellent integral luggage capacity.

HONDA V-FOUR

The Honda V-Four family did not get off to the best of starts. The Japanese manufacturer introduced the first mass-produced V4 motorcycle in 1982, but, as one commentator rightly said, "the 750S was met with all the enthusiasm one accords to cold porridge." Unfortunately, the machine's revolutionary engine was compromised by appalling styling, a bad riding position, and poor handling.

THE VF 750F

A year later, Honda introduced the VF 750F (Interceptor in the USA), a super sport version of the original, which performed, handled, and looked much better. It promptly outsold every other 750 that year. Unfortunately, the "F" was plagued by mechanical woes, which largely centred on camshaft wear and cam chains. By this time, Honda had extended its V4 range to include 400, 500, and 1,000cc models, the last in two guises – roadster and race replica. The public, however, had lost faith in the concept.

PUTTING THINGS RIGHT

Unused to such a humiliating response, Honda re-examined and revised the design, launching the VFR750 in 1985. In the process, it not only reinvented the V4 configuration, but also produced an all-time great. The VFR (which featured gear-driven cams) was an all-rounder, however, not a true sports bike. To fill this role, the company went a stage farther and created the RC (Racing Corporation) sports/racing machines. Subsequently, examples of these bikes gained four World Superbike titles and proved to be Japan's main challengers to the all-conquering Ducatis during the first decade of the championship series.

RC30 AND RC45

Launched in 1988, the Honda RC30 was a genuine racer that could also serve as a street bike. Its 749.2cc, liquid-cooled, double-overhead-camshaft, 90-degree V4 engine generated 103bhp at 11,500rpm and could push the bike to 246km/h (153mph) in full road trim.

Production of the RC30 ended in 1992. It was replaced by the RC45, which was offered from 1994 to 1998. The new model copied the RC30 in many respects, including the engine size, aluminium frame, and revolutionary, single-sided rear swinging arm, which had been developed in conjunction with the French ELF company. The RC45 was lighter than the RC30, however, at 189kg (416.6lb) compared with the latter's 193kg (425.4lb).

Among the features carried over from the earlier machine were lightweight titanium con-rods, but the RC45 employed new powder-metal composite cylinder liners (the RC30 had steel items). There were also improvements to the six-speed gearbox, hydraulic clutch, and cooling system, and a revised four-into-one exhaust. The new bike was equipped with programmed fuel injection, a first on a production Honda. An inverted front fork replaced the conventional telescopic unit of the RC30, while the swinging arm was modified to accommodate a wider tyre.

facing page Carl Fogarty (1) and Arron Slight (3) with their Castrol-sponsored, works RC45 V4s, circa 1996.

above Launched in 1986, the RC30 was a genuine racer that could double as a road bike.

right The RC30's 749.2cc, liquid-cooled, double-overhead-camshaft, 90-degree V4 put out 103bhp at 11,500rpm.

below Honda also produced a series of other V4 designs, including the VF400 of 1984.

below right A feature of the RC30 (and RC45) was the French ELF-conceived, single-sided, rear swinging arm.

AERODYNAMICS

The development of the modern, high-performance motorcycle has been greatly assisted by the incredible strides made in aerodynamic streamlining over the past few decades. Initially, streamlining was employed in motorcycle speed record attempts, then was adopted for racing machines, and finally made an appearance on production roadsters. Although several motorcycle designs had some form of enclosure before World War II, proper streamlining did not become commonplace until the 1950s.

GRAND PRIX

It was in grand prix racing that the use of streamlining really flourished. At the beginning of the 1950s, machines had simple flyscreens, but by the middle of the decade, full "dustbin" fairings were the rule. Concerned that the practice was getting out of hand, the sport's governing body, the FIM, banned full streamlining – on safety grounds – from the end of the 1957 season.

From the beginning of 1958, racing machines began using the "dolphin" fairing, a much less cumbersome device than the fully streamlined "dustbin" shell of the previous year. Even today, the "dolphin" is the only form of fairing used on racing machines; it is also fitted to production street bikes. Although far from perfect, it does not suffer from problems in high side winds, which caused the "dustbin" to be banned.

THE FIRST "PRODUCTION" FAIRINGS

The first fairings to be fitted to production roadsters, as original equipment, were largely the work of British motorcycle manufacturers. In 1955, Vincent introduced the fully faired Black Knight V-twin; other notable examples, which appeared at the end of that decade, were the Royal Enfield Airflow and the Ariel Leader.

During the mid-1970s, BMW (R100RS) and Moto Guzzi (SP1000) offered faired machines, being joined, in 1979, by Ducati (Mike Hailwood Replica). For once, the Japanese had been caught off guard – even as the 1980s dawned, most of their machines were still "naked".

facing page With their low lines, kneeler racing sidecar machines display good aerodynamics.

right On the 2005 Ducati 999, the rear silencer was faired-in to improve streamlining.

below The 2003 Benelli 900 Tornado triple incorporated air ducts for the cooling and fuel injection systems.

below right The narrow frontal view of Kawasaki's GPZ600R, which was the first of the 600 super sport machines.

With the advent of the racer replica (such as the Suzuki GSX-R750) and tourer (Kawasaki GTR), however, the Japanese had soon covered up most of their bikes.

BETTER PERFORMANCE AND FUEL ECONOMY

Today, streamlining is a vital feature of motorcycle design. Not only does it improve rider comfort and machine aesthetics, but it also offers gains in performance and fuel economy. Key aims in a design team's mission are minimal frontal projected area and coefficient of drag (CdA). At around 200 km/h (125 mph), reducing the CdA of a bike by only 0.01 adds 1 km/h (0.62 mph) to the speed – equivalent to raising engine power by 1–2 bhp. At higher speeds, the increase is substantially greater. Thus, as speeds rise, aerodynamics become ever more important.

The engine of a modern streamlined motorcycle requires a good supply of cooling air to prevent overheating. Ducts to allow this to enter and escape are built into the front, sides, and rear of the fairing.

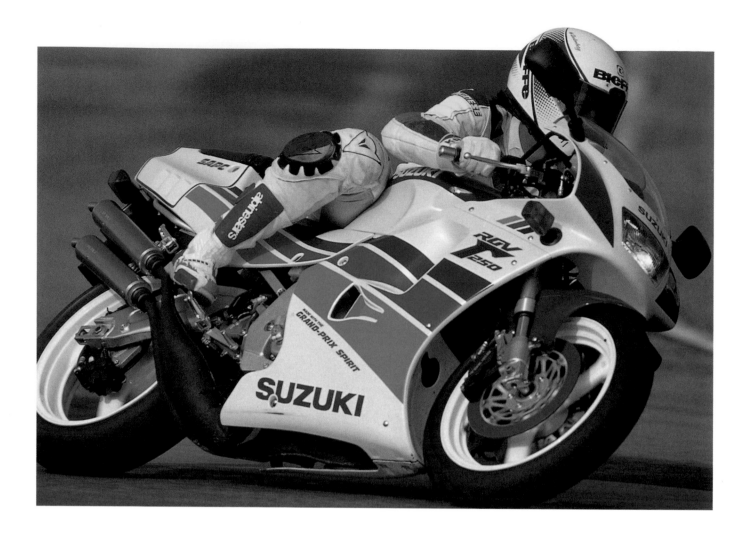

SUZUKI RGV250

During the late 1980s and early 1990s, the Suzuki RGV250 V-twin was one of the most popular motorcycles. The key to its success was its unique blend of high performance, race-like handling, and relatively low purchase price.

The origins of the design can be traced back to 1983, when Suzuki introduced its excellent RG250 parallel twin. Although this never sold in large numbers, it was the best-handling Japanese bike of its era. Not only did it pioneer the use of single-shock, rising-rate rear suspension in Suzuki's range, but it also displaced the Yamaha 250LC as the top production racer in the 250cc class.

THE RGV250 ARRIVES

The first news of the RG250's replacement came in early 1987, when details of a sensational new Suzuki 250 leaked out; it went on sale later that year. The first version to be exported was the "K", in the 1989 model year. This was followed in 1990 by the "L", which was virtually identical.

The "K" and "L" versions of the RGV250 had the same 249cc, 90-degree, V-twin engine, equipped with twin Slingshot carburettors, a newly designed induction system, a radial-flow radiator, and automatic exhaust timing control (AETC) to increase torque throughout the rev range. The result (with full road silencing) was a power output of 57 bhp at 11,000 rpm and a top speed of 209 km/h (130 mph).

ALLOY FRAME

Made from cast alloy, the RGV250's frame had been designed to minimize weight while maintaining torsional strength. It was equipped with Suzuki's "full-floater", link-type, monoshock rear suspension and triple disc brakes.

Unfortunately, the early RGV models were not particularly reliable, suffering from seized power valves, and cylinder and piston problems. Suzuki engineers tackled these shortcomings for the 1991 model year, when they virtually redesigned the RGV. The result was a much better bike with an uprated engine that featured new power valves. There was also a crescent-shaped, aluminium, rear swinging arm. This allowed both expansion-chamber exhaust outlets to discharge on the right and also permitted an amazing 58-degree banking angle.

facing page The RGV250 was uprated for 1991 as the "M".

below The 1989 ("K") and 1990 ("L") versions of the RGV250 were virtually identical.

Other developments included a coaxially mounted gear-shift lever and revised gear ratios to improve acceleration. The main frame was strengthened as well.

INVERTED FRONT FORK

The new bike featured an inverted (upside-down) front fork with a revised steering-head angle. The wheel size was 432mm (17in) front and rear (previously, an 457mm/18in rear wheel had been used), while the brakes were uprated.

Although the power output remained unchanged, a reprogrammed engine management system provided more usable power characteristics. Suzuki also offered a wide range of racing parts in "kit" form. These included close-ratio gear sets (a cassette gear cluster was employed), power-valve breathers, full racing exhausts, and a racing engine management "black box".

With kit parts and specialized tuning, 70bhp was possible, and for several years the RGV was "top dog" in the highly competitive Super Sport 400 class (250cc two-strokes; 400cc four-strokes).

1989 SUZUKI RGV250K
SPECIFICATIONS

Engine Liquid-cooled, reed-valve, two-stroke, 90-degree, V-twin

Displacement 249cc

Bore and stroke 54.0x54.0mm

Ignition Electronic

Gearbox Six-speed, foot-change

Final drive Chain

Frame Aluminium, Deltabox

Dry weight 128kg (282lb)

Maximum power 57bhp at 11,000rpm

Top speed 209km/h (130mph)

HONDA FIREBLADE

Two motorcycles dominated the sports-bike scene during the 1990s: the fabulous Ducati 916 and Honda's equally brilliant CBR900RR FireBlade.

GETTING IN FIRST

Arriving first, in 1992, the FireBlade immediately put its rivals at a disadvantage with its combination of very light weight and stunning power. Honda's engineering team, led by Tadeo Baba, had conceived an 893cc, liquid-cooled, double-overhead-camshaft, 16-valve, across-the-frame four, which, in its original "N" guise, developed 122bhp at 10,500rpm, giving a top speed of 266km/h (165mph). With its low 186.5kg (411lb) weight, the machine's power-to-weight ratio was unmatched.

Only the sub-900cc engine size was questioned, but this was rectified when increased to 918cc for 1996, then 929cc for 2000, and 998cc for 2004.

QUEST FOR MINIMUM WEIGHT

The FireBlade's impressive technical specification, for a series-production bike, helps to explain why the power-to-weight ratio was so good. Baba and his team had set out to create a no-compromise sportster in the quest for minimum weight.

Flat-topped, ultra-lightweight slipper pistons gave a high degree of rigidity, while equally lightweight con-rods and crankshaft minimized inertia and provided an extremely crisp engine response. Another weight-saving measure was the use of magnesium instead of aluminium for the cylinder head (from the 1994 model year).

The FireBlade's 16 valves were operated directly by twin camshafts, resulting in a compact, low-friction valve-train. This required adjustment only every 25,700km (16,000 miles).

CARBURETTORS TO FUEL INJECTION

Originally, a bank of four 38mm, flat-slide carburettors fed the engine with fuel through a single-port induction system. But from 2000, an electronically controlled, PGM-F1 fuel injection system did this task, giving a more precise throttle response.

A cartridge-type, liquid-cooled oil cooler was fitted to keep lubricant temperatures under control for stable output and maximum engine life.

ALUMINIUM FRAME

The chassis played a vital role in the FireBlade's success and was subjected to a steady evolutionary process. From the very beginning, in 1992, it was made of aluminium. By the 1997 model, the frame was based on two main spars of extruded aluminium, weighing a mere 10.5 kg (23 lb). Featuring a semi-floating rubber engine mount to combat vibration, it supported an aluminium, rear swinging arm that had been designed with the aid of computer analysis and rigorous track testing.

For 2000, radical changes were made to the FireBlade. In addition to the fuel injection system, there was the larger (929 cc) engine size, a longer rear swinging arm, larger front brake discs, and inverted front fork (a first for Honda's big-bore sports models). To enable the machine to compete in the revised World Superbike series, Honda increased the engine size to 998 cc for 2004.

2000 HONDA FIREBLADE
SPECIFICATIONS

Engine Liquid-cooled, double-overhead-camshaft, 16-valve, across-the-frame, four-cylinder

Displacement 929 cc

Bore and stroke 74.0 x 54.0 mm

Ignition Digital with integrated fuel injection

Gearbox Six-speed, foot-change

Final drive Chain

Frame Aluminium, triple box spars, multi-point diamond configuration

Dry weight 170 kg (373.7 lb)

Maximum power 152 bhp at 11,000 rpm

Top speed 273.5 km/h (170 mph)

9 LIFESTYL

E AND
LEISURE

left John Bloor had the foresight to purchase the Triumph name when the Meriden factory closed in the early 1980s. A decade later, the first of the marque's new models appeared. A 2005 Legend is shown.

below Another marque that has done well in recent times is the Italian Ducati concern. One of its best sellers has been the Monster, launched in 1993. This is a 2004 S2R.

facing page Kawasaki's VN800 is a typical cruiser, affording its rider the chance to see the countryside in style.

LIFESTYLE AND LEISURE

By the beginning of the 21st century, the motorcycle was no longer seen primarily as a means of transport, rather it had become an aspect of lifestyle and leisure. The latest designs and innovations would have seemed as remote as the prospect of space travel 100 years ago, at the dawn of the internal-combustion engine and the first motorcycles.

Not only has the whole purpose of the motorcycle changed, but also the technology behind it. Today, like cars, motorcycles are no longer constructed in a manner that allows them to be serviced by the home mechanic. Instead, complex computerized systems govern many of the operations. This is due to both technical advances and changes in the industry, where dealer servicing has become the norm, with attendant commercial benefits. The situation also goes some way to explaining why classic bikes have become so

popular – as a rule, a motorcycle manufactured before the end of the 1970s can be rebuilt by a knowledgeable enthusiast with only limited workshop facilities. With the advent of such features as solid-state electrics, digital ignition, and fuel injection, however, even a conventional workshop manual is no longer of use; the skilled mechanic has been replaced by the computer.

Moreover, the industry makes far more specialized machines. In the past, manufacturers built a single model that could cope with many tasks, such as commuting, touring, clubman's racing, and even off-road forays. That is no longer the case.

Today, the motorcycle market has defined sectors: sports bikes (many of which require little modification to go racing), tourers, enduro-styled on/off-roaders, custom cruisers, retro-styled machines, motocrossers, scooters, trials bikes, and superbikes. Whatever your requirements, there is a bike designed specifically to meet that need.

It would be true to say that no bad motorcycles are manufactured today; something that certainly could not have been said even 20 years ago.

The renowned American manufacturer Harley-Davidson really started the "lifestyle" culture in motorcycling. Other marques have followed the company's lead, with varying degrees of success.

But what of the future? Well, safety is certain to become more of an issue than it is today. Already, experiments have been carried out with leg protectors and even air bags on motorcycles. BMW attempted to set an example with a self-imposed 100bhp engine power limit in

the 1980s and 1990s but, since then, has been forced to join the power race. As engine sizes and power outputs creep ever higher, it may only be a matter of time before governments step in and call a halt through legislation. Perhaps smaller-capacity, more fuel-efficient motorcycles will make a return sometime in the near future.

These and other important issues that affect motorcycle design are already being studied by manufacturers' engineering teams around the world.

Finally, it is interesting to speculate on which nation will be the next major motorcycle power – China maybe?

CUSTOM BIKES

The factory-built custom bike owes its existence, primarily, to the 1976 film *Easy Rider*. Featuring a pair of "chopped" Harley-Davidsons, breathtaking American landscapes and contemporary sound track, the movie caused a whole generation to become converts to a new motorcycle sub-culture, almost overnight. It encouraged fantasies of the custom-cruiser life, wherein the sun always shone, the air was clean, and the highway stretched, arrow-straight, as far as the eye could see.

At first, many enthusiasts "chopped" existing motorcycles. A whole new cottage industry was established (in similar fashion to the earlier café racer cult) to meet their needs, producing everything from "King and Queen" seats through "peanut" tanks to complete bikes, and even trikes.

Harley-Davidson has benefited substantially from building bikes that reflect the custom-cruiser lifestyle image, as have Honda, Kawasaki, Yamaha, and Suzuki. All four Japanese marques have produced myriad Harley-like V-twins, ranging from the small to the truly massive. BMW has also muscled into the act with its R1200C (Custom) flat-twin cruiser.

YAMAHA XV535 VIRAGO

Yamaha's XV535 Virago was a brilliant design. For years, the Japanese manufacturers had tried everything to produce a top-selling custom bike, but with little success. The XV535 changed all that. Introduced at the end of the 1980s, it remained a popular bike in the early years of the 21st century. Developing 47 bhp, its single-overhead-camshaft, V-twin engine could propel the machine to a genuine 160 km/h (100 mph). With a choice of flat or pull-back handlebars, shaft final drive, front disc brake (rear drum), a dry weight of 182 kg (401 lb), it was very easy to ride. As a result, it was responsible for introducing many newcomers to biking – and for encouraging more than a few ex-motorcyclists to return.

HONDA VTX1800

The much more recent Honda VTX1800 was right at the other end of the custom-cruiser spectrum. This monster was powered by a liquid-cooled, single-overhead-camshaft, six-valve, 52-degree V-twin. It displayed a combination of technical innovation and traditional approach in its design. For example, at the front, it had an inverted fork and six brake caliper pistons, while at the rear were two fully enclosed, chromed shocks. Weighing in at a hefty 321 kg (708 lb), the VTX produced 95 bhp at 5,000 rpm.

BMW R1200C

As might be expected, the R1200C had BMW's characteristic flat-twin engine. At the time of its launch, in 1998, the 1,170 cc (101.0 x 73.0 mm bore and stroke), four-valves-per-cylinder, high-camshaft unit was the largest of its type produced by the German marque. The machine not only employed the latest Motronic engine management system, but was also the first custom cruiser to feature exhaust emission control by closed-loop, three-way catalytic converter as standard.

left Honda's VTX1800 has masses of chrome-plated components, including the engine outer covers, the exhaust and air cleaner. It is a massive machine, weighing 321 kg (708 lb).

below The 2005 VTX1800 has an advanced specification, which includes a liquid-cooled, six-valve, 52-degree, V-twin engine.

facing page A pair of Kawasaki Eliminator 600s. Excellent performance came from a detuned ZZR four-cylinder engine and relatively light weight.

below BMW's R1200C was the first custom model from the famous German marque. It was a high-quality product with a 1,170cc, four-valves-per-cylinder, high-camshaft, flat-twin power unit.

CUSTOM BIKES   **199**

RETRO BIKES

The retro bike combines "yesteryear" looks (without the all-enveloping plastic bodywork of most modern machines), the latest technology, and a "street fighter" image.

BIRTH OF THE CONCEPT

Today, retro bikes occupy an important sector of the market. This style of machine was conceived during the late 1980s, when the Italian Moto Guzzi company launched the nostalgic 1000S. This newcomer differed from its contemporaries in that it clearly aped the classic 750S3 model of the early 1970s, but with an updated specification.

Perhaps without realizing it, the long-established Italian marque had created an entirely new breed of motorcycle, the retro model. The dictionary defines the word "retrospect" as

"when you look back", which is exactly what Guzzi had done. "Retrospect" hardly trips off the tongue, however, so the industry's marketing men shortened it to "retro". Since then, many retro machines have been performance orientated, not simply rehashes of old favourites, and usually the engineering has been bang up to date.

THE ZEPHYR

The first Japanese company to exploit the retro concept was Kawasaki, with its Zephyr series, initially a Japanese-market-only 400, which was introduced in 1989. A larger-engined model arrived in 1990, basically the same machine bored and stroked to 553cc; later still came the 750 and 1,000 Zephyrs. All copied the high-performance, air-cooled Kawasaki

facing page A 1999 Laverda 750 Strike. It's retro styling hid an advanced specification, which included a double-overhead-camshaft, parallel twin engine, six speeds, inverted front fork and aluminium, twin-spar frame.

left Kawasaki's Zephyr 550 was introduced in Japan and the USA in 1990, and in Europe in 1991. It is largely credited with starting the retro fashion.

below Two of the most popular retros of 2005, the Triumph Bonneville (left) and Kawasaki W650. Both had parallel twin engines, the British bike's being an overhead-valve unit, while the Japanese machine had an overhead camshaft.

fours of the previous two decades, and specifically the 1000R Eddie Lawson Replica, "arguably Kawasaki's ultimate hot rod", as *Cycle* magazine reported in its 1990 road test of the 550 Zephyr. Later in the decade, Kawasaki ditched the Zephyr series in favour of the excellent "pure classic" W650 twin. This looked like a 1960 Triumph Bonneville, but came with an eight-valve, overhead-cam engine, electric starter, digital ignition, five-speed gearbox, and front disc brake.

SUZUKI BANDIT

Although Suzuki was the last to enter the retro market, it was certainly the most successful, with its outstanding 600 Bandit (1995) and 1,200 Bandit (1996). Both became top sellers – on merit. Compared with the earlier Japanese retros, the

Bandit models scored by having modern, single-shock rear suspension, while their rivals retained the old-fashioned, "classic" twin-shock arrangement. The Suzukis also gained by being much lighter in weight.

THE EUROPEAN RESPONSE

In addition to the reborn British Triumph marque, which launched its Bonneville retro in 2000, BMW, Laverda, and Ducati have all produced their own interpretations of the theme. Like the Suzuki, the Ducati Monster proved a hit. Designed by Miguel Angel Galluzzi, it was introduced at the Cologne motorcycle show in late 1992. Subsequently, it was produced in 600, 750, 900, and 1,000 engine sizes, in both two- and four-valves-per-cylinder guises.

DUCATI

For almost three decades, the design talents of Fabio Taglioni had guided Ducati. He had been responsible for creating the singles and V-twins that had established the Italian company as a household name among motorcyclists.

FOUR-VALVE TECHNOLOGY

Taglioni, however, had chosen largely to ignore the development potential of four-valve technology. This was left to his successor, Massimo Bordi.

The first of Bordi's four-valves-per-cylinder models made its debut in 1986 at the French Bol d'Or 24-hour endurance event. Although it retired after running for eight hours, it had shown great potential.

The Cagiva takeover of Ducati in 1985 had provided the funding for the project, and the first production model, the 851, arrived in 1988. In the same year, Marco Lucchinelli used the bike to win the first ever World Superbike race at the British Donington Park circuit.

The standard 851 had bore and stroke dimensions of 92.0x64.0mm, but the bore in Lucchinelli's bike measured 94.0mm, giving 888cc.

Ducati won its initial World Superbike title in 1990 (the first of a series) with Raymond Roche. The company built the 851 and later 888 models for sale as both racers and street bikes, one of them being the limited-edition SP (Sport Production). The 851 was discontinued in 1993, and in 1994, the Corsa (Racing) model's engine size was increased to 926cc.

THE 916

The really big news for 1994, however, was the arrival of the ground-breaking 916. This machine's engine size matched its code number and had been achieved by increasing the stroke of the 888 from 64 to 66mm.

The remainder of the 916, though, set it apart from earlier Ducatis. This was the work of Massimo Tamburini, who has been described as one of the greatest motorcycle designers of the late 20th century – and with good cause.

To many enthusiasts around the world, the 916 was not simply the latest superbike, but the best there had ever been. It set new standards of performance, handling, and braking, but also had style and charisma. The choice of a Ferrari-red paint scheme added to the overall effect, as did the twin-head-lamp fairing, high-level silencers, single-sided, rear swinging arm, and magical, deep-throated, booming exhaust note.

996, 998, AND 999

The 916 changed the face of sports bikes in a way that only the original Suzuki GSX-R750 had managed a decade earlier.

To further improve its chances, Ducati employed a 996cc (98.0x66.0mm bore and stroke) engine in its World Superbike racers – and, from 1999, in its series-production roadsters. Later, this was enlarged even more, to 998cc, before, in 2004, being replaced by the Pierre Terblance-styled 999. For many enthusiasts, however, the Tamburini styling of the 916/996 era was best.

left Introduced in 1987, the Ducati 851 V-twin was the first of the marque's bikes to feature four valves per cylinder, liquid cooling, and fuel injection. The 888 followed; this is a 1993 SP5 model.

facing page:
top The Ducati 916 replaced the 888 and had all-new styling.

bottom Ducati dominated the World Superbike series during the 1990s with the 916 and, later, the 996.

HARLEY-DAVIDSON: THE MODERN ERA

Harley-Davidson motorcycles – like Porsches in the car world – are shining examples of how a primitive design can be refined until it is comparable with many, much more technically advanced machines. Also, like the renowned German cars, Harley-Davidsons are considered icons.

For some of its 100-plus-year history, however, Harley-Davidson didn't enjoy the reverence it receives today. During that period (1968–81), the marque was under the control of the American Machine & Foundry Company (AMF).

THE AMF TAKEOVER

Formed in 1903, Harley-Davidson remained a family dominated business until it became a public-owned company in 1965. In 1968, it was taken over by AMF, which, although willing to invest large sums of money, unfortunately didn't understand the motorcycle business. This resulted in poor-quality products and lacklustre marketing. Not surprisingly, the company's market share fell while losses rose. Finally, during 1981–82, a management buy-out took place, which brought a revival of the famous marque's fortunes.

"NEW NOSTALGIA"

One of the main facets of the revival plan would become known as "new nostalgia", the machines' somewhat "dated" looks being emphasized as a positive asset. This trend-setting idea was inspired by Willie G. Davidson and led to Harley-Davidson's V-twin street bikes being promoted as the motorcycles to be seen on. This was helped by the fact that many famous personalities – film stars, sportsmen, and even politicians – became Harley owners.

In a clever marketing ploy, the company created a whole family of nostalgically styled V-twins, among them the 883 Sportster, XL1200 Sportster Custom, FXDL Road King (based on the long-running Electra Glide), and the FLSTCN Heritage Softail Special. All had variations of the legendary 45-degree, V-twin engine, which had been given a major facelift as the V2 Evolution in the mid-1980s.

This was a classic Harley-Davidson update, not a back-to-the-drawing-board (or computer, as it is now) project. Although the old and the new engines look similar externally, the latter was improved in almost every aspect. For example, the alloy cylinder barrels with iron liners were far more efficient at removing excess heat. The entire engine was lighter, more powerful and easier to maintain.

THE ACCESSORY MARKET

Harley's biggest success, however, has been its ability to encourage many owners to personalize their bikes with after-market accessories. In fact, the commercial success enjoyed by the company since the mid-1980s has been built on this strategy. This is where the real profits have been generated and why Harley-Davidson has managed to grow year-on-year in such a storming fashion, with bikes that are based on what is, essentially, an outdated design.

left Designed as the most affordable of the modern Harley-Davidsons, the 883 model allowed owners to benefit from the aura surrounding the famous American marque.

facing page:

top In the early 21st century, Harley-Davidson introduced the liquid-cooled, 1,130cc, VRSCA V-Rod, with 115bhp and a top speed of 216km/h (134mph).

bottom Buell is the sports-bike division of Harley-Davidson, former racer Erik Buell being responsible for the lightweight, monoshock chassis design.

OFF-ROAD RACERS

Off-road racing has boomed in recent years. It is an exciting sport for riders and spectators alike; with the steady growth in leisure time and living standards, many have been encouraged to take it up.

Although European marques, among them KTM and Husqvarna, are still involved, the Japanese manufacturers have made much of the recent running. Honda, for example, offers a vast range of off-road machinery, ranging from the CRF50F (with 49.4 cc, single-overhead-camshaft, two-valve horizontal single) to range-topping models such as the XR650R (enduro), CRF 450x (motocross), and the FMX 650 (which Honda classifies as "Adventure", but is actually a Super Motad racer).

AN ALUMINIUM CHASSIS
In 1997, Honda took motocross technology into a new era, at least as far as production models were concerned, when it introduced its CR250. This had a trend-setting, aluminium, twin-spar frame, which set it apart from the competition.

In preceding years, there had been a host of important developments. These included advances in two-stroke technology (such as reed and power valves, liquid cooling and map-type, digital electronic ignition), five- and six-speed gearboxes, aluminium swinging arms, rising-rate, single-shock rear suspension, front and rear disc brakes, inverted front forks, and plastic bodywork.

In addition to its aluminium frame, the CR250 had a 249 cc (66.4x72.0mm bore and stroke), two-stroke, single-cylinder engine with a composite racing valve (CRV), an all-new power-jet-control (PJC) carburettor and a host of other improvements compared with earlier versions.

By 2005, the CR250 generated 58 bhp at 8,000 rpm. It had been joined by the CRF250 with a 249.4 cc, liquid-cooled, single-overhead-camshaft, four-valve, four-stroke engine.

FOUR-STROKES
At the beginning of the 21st century, the previously dominant two-stroke was supplemented by a new breed of high-performance, high-tech, four-stroke, off-road racer. Honda offered 50, 70, 100, 250, 450, and 650 models, the last for enduro and Super Motad events.

New for 2005 was the road-legal FMX650, with a 644 cc, air-cooled, single-overhead-camshaft engine that produced 37 bhp at 5,750 rpm. The equally new CRF450x was a genuine motocross racer, displacing 449 cc, with liquid cooling, four valves, and single overhead camshaft. Honda claimed a power output of 48.5 bhp at 7,500 rpm.

The most amazing machine in the 2005 Honda off-road line-up, however, was the CR125R. Its liquid-cooled, single-cylinder, two-stroke engine put out an amazing 42 bhp at a screaming 11,500 rpm.

facing page Part of an impressive line-up of high-tech dirt bikes from Honda for 2005. Left to right: TRM Super Moto, FMX650 and CRF450R.

above The FMX650 644cc, air-cooled, single-overhead-camshaft, single-cylinder engine with dual exhaust ports produced 37 bhp at 5,750 rpm.

left Motocross champion and Kawasaki works rider Kurt Nichols, with a KM5000 dirt racer powered by a liquid-cooled, reed-valve, two-stroke motor.

V-TWINS

V-twin engines have been around since the dawn of motor-cycling, but the latest examples are very sophisticated, and most offer breathtaking performance. In fact, modern V-twins are so good that, in recent years, bikes such as the Aprilia RSV Mille, Honda VTR 1000 SP-2 and Firestorm, Suzuki TL1000, French Voxon, Ducati 999, and Yamaha MT-01 are comparable to the best of the multi-cylinder machines.

THE REBIRTH

Many of the classic V-twin bikes, such as the Brough Superior and Vincent, are the top icons of their eras. Production of the Brough ended in 1939, of course, and the Vincent in 1955. In the old days, the angle between the cylinders could be anything from almost zero (Matchless Silver Arrow) to 120 degrees (as was the case in the Moto Guzzi 500 racer ridden to victory by Stanley Woods in the 1935 Senior TT).

Ducati's Fabio Taglioni laid the groundwork for the modern V-twin, certainly as regards high-performance sports models. His successor, Massimo Bordi, took things a stage farther with liquid cooling, the use of four valves per cylinder and, most importantly, an integrated electronic fuel injection and ignition system developed in conjunction with Weber-Marelli.

THE APRILIA

The Aprilia RSV differed considerably from Ducati's V-series. For a start, it had a narrower angle between the cylinders – 60 degrees instead of 90. At the time of its launch in 1998, Georgio del Ton, Aprilia's head of engine development, said, "With everyone else jumping on the 90-degree bandwagon (Honda and Suzuki, for example), we felt it necessary to establish our own identity. We compared both layouts carefully. The 90-degree engine has many advantages, but we felt there were too many compromises with its design when building a lightweight, compact, sporting motorcycle. For example, we were able to keep the RSV's wheelbase in check without resort-ing to trick alternative rear shocks and side-mounted radiators. It also allowed us to keep fuel injection components close together, which is critical to allowing straight, short inlet tracts for the cylinder heads." Another departure from the Ducati formula was the use of dry- rather than wet-sump lubrication.

YAMAHA

During the early 1980s, Yamaha marketed the 981cc TR1, which employed a 75-degree, overhead-camshaft V-twin, and had single-shock rear suspension. This never sold well, however, and eventually it was dropped from the range.

Then, in 2005, the Japanese marque launched the incred-ible 1,670cc MT-01. Featuring a big-bore, long-stroke engine with stunning high-torque thrust, it bristled with innovations. Among these were digital fuel injection; forged pistons and ceramic-coated cylinders; a fully adjustable, 43mm, inverted front fork; an alloy frame; and an R1-derived, truss-style, rear swinging arm.

In the MT-01, with its jaw-dropping performance, the long-running V-twin concept had been more than simply modernized – it had been redrawn completely.

facing page:

left Cagiva's Gran Canyon had an air-cooled Ducati 900SS engine (shown) initially, and from 2000, a Suzuki TL1000 unit. Both were 90-degree V-twins.

right The Aprilia RSV Mille, equipped with a liquid-cooled, double-overhead-camshaft, 60-degree, V-twin engine. The camshaft drive combined chains and gears.

top left and right Features of the 2005 Yamaha MT-01: matching, white-faced instruments (left); and futuristic headlamp design.

above The MT-01 was powered by a 1,670cc, overhead-valve, V-twin engine with four valves per cylinder, fuel injection, and dry-sump lubrication.

left The Voxon was yet another new breed of V-twin, offering excellent performance, plenty of torque, and unique styling.

COLOUR CODING

During the early decades of motorcycling, bikes were usually finished in drab colour schemes – black and dark greens, reds or blues. Then, toward the end of the 1950s, the Italian manufacturers began to give their sporting lightweights eye-catching finishes. Ducati (and others), for example, sold machines with gold frames and metallic cherry red tanks, side panels and mudguards.

COLOURED LEATHERS

In the mid-1960s, racers began wearing coloured leathers – before, they had been universally black. This fashion had its roots in the United States, but was soon taken up in Europe, where the Englishman Rod Scivyer gained more fame by wearing a set of white leathers than he did by winning the 125 cc British Road Racing Championship title.

In the 1970s, with the dawn of the superbike era, colour coding began to take hold as riders, particularly in the USA and Germany, began matching their riding gear to their bikes.

THE MANUFACTURERS CATCH ON

At first, coloured leathers, boots, and gloves had to be made individually by specialists. As the 1970s gave way to the 1980s, however, motorcycle manufacturers such as Honda, Kawasaki, Suzuki, and Yamaha began to appreciate that they could benefit by meeting this new demand. Not only was there

money to be made from the sale of such clothing, but also free advertising to be gained from the addition of their logos.

Kawasaki began finishing its bikes in a shocking bright green livery, which proved a great success. As a result, its factory racers, motocrossers, and road bikes established the marque's famous "Mean Green" nickname.

MOBILE BILLBOARDS

As riders and bikes became increasingly colourful, so they became adorned with sponsors' logos. Prior to the 1970s, racing machines and their riders did not carry any kind of corporate badging. By the late 1970s, however, they had begun to resemble advertising billboards. Today, this is accepted as the norm, prompted by the television coverage of such events as Moto GP and World Superbike racing.

IMITATION

Many of today's riders of road bikes are keen to exploit this "branding", not only to re-create the image that their racing heroes portray on the track, but also to share in the brand image, whether it be Honda, Suzuki, Yamaha, Kawasaki, Ducati, Triumph, or the like. This in turn has provided a ready market for identical colourful bike liveries, riding gear, and associated items. Manufacturers are more than happy to meet this demand.

facing page Colour coding applies not only to the motorcycle, but also to the modern rider's gear.

right Moto GP rider Alex Barros (4) with his factory-backed Honda during the 2005 season, displaying his distinctive yellow and blue colours.

below World Champion Valentino Rossi (46, Yamaha) leads Ducati's Loris Capirossi. The Japanese marque's red and white scheme makes a striking contrast to the Italian bike's all-red livery.

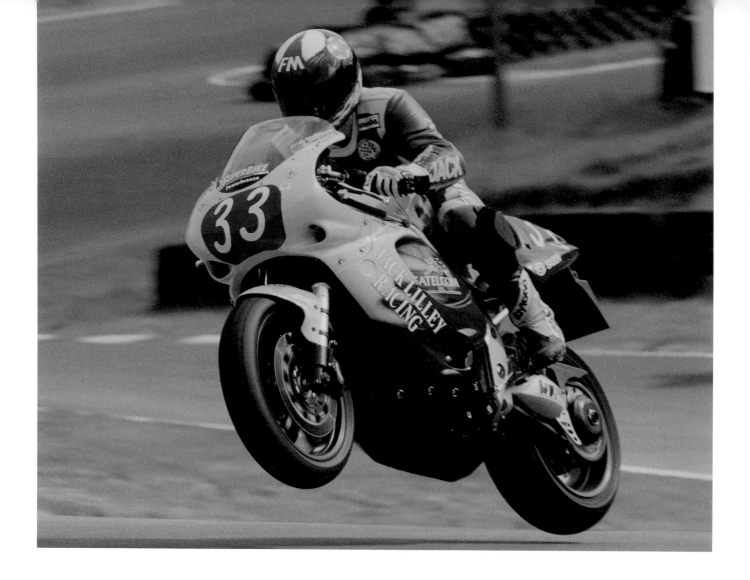

TRIUMPH REBORN

One of the real success stories of recent times is Triumph's revival under its new owner, John Bloor. The famous British marque's range of three- and four-cylinder bikes has successfully challenged the best that Japan has to offer in the showrooms – and on the road.

After buying the rights to the Triumph name in the early 1980s, Bloor brought the project to life at the Cologne motorcycle show in September 1990. By 1996, a new Triumph was rolling off the production line every six minutes, giving an annual production figure of 15,000 machines. Since then, output has risen dramatically. Today, Triumphs are exported to such diverse destinations as Australia, Brazil, Kuwait, Mexico, Russia, and Taiwan, as well as North America and Europe.

The 2005 Triumph range included machines labelled Cruisers, Urban Sports, and Modern Classics.

THE AMAZING ROCKET III

A few years ago, any kind of cruiser with the sheer size and performance of the Rocket III would have been an impossible dream. Triumph, however, made that dream an awesome reality.

The machine's three inline, fuel-injected cylinders displaced a massive 2,294cc, and produced 140bhp and 219kg/m (147lb/ft) of torque. This output was fed to a giant, 240-section tyre through a five-speed gearbox and shaft final drive. Keeping all that power under control was an extremely strong, steel frame, inverted front fork, twin rear shocks, and triple disc brakes with four-piston calipers from the marque's 955i sportster. Other engine features included double overhead camshafts and digital ignition. All things considered, its weight of 320kg (704lb) was less than might have been expected.

SPEED TRIPLE

The Speed Triple was introduced in the mid-1990s and, subsequently, was updated considerably. It was given a new 1,050cc, across-the-frame, three-cylinder engine, which provided plenty of power (128bhp) and excellent torque. Along with the bigger engine came a new gearbox with improved

T509 SPEED triple

facing page Under the ownership of John Bloor, Triumph re-established itself as a leading motorcycle marque during the late 1990s and early 21st century. Here, Francis Williamson crests the famous Mountain at Cadwell Park on a T595 triple, circa 1998.

right A 2005 Triumph T509 Speed Triple.

below With its 2,294cc, fuel-injected, three-cylinder engine, Triumph's Rocket III is "King of the Cruisers".

below right Triumph's styling studio came up with this striking rendition of the British Union Jack flag.

action. There was also a new aluminium frame, fully adjustable, inverted front fork, and a remote-reservoir, rear monoshock. The "street fighter" style that made the Speed Triple so popular, however, was retained.

THRUXTON 900

Triumph launched its new "classic" Bonneville 790cc, air-cooled, vertical twin in 2001. Four years later, it created the Thruxton 900, with a tuned and bored (from 86 to 90mm) version of the existing Bonneville motor. The newcomer was particularly successful in recapturing the spirit and style of the 1960s café racer era. With clip-on handlebars, rear-set footrests, twin upswept megaphone silencers, chrome head-lamp, and evocative seat hump, it couldn't help but impress potential buyers.

In the early 21st century, with a range that encompassed super sports machines, tourers, trail bikes, and cruisers, the reborn Triumph marque was back among the leaders in motorcycle design.

YAMAHA R1

When it appeared at the end of 1997, the Yamaha R1 caused a sensation. The 1,000cc bike, in full road trim, weighed an amazingly low 177kg (390lb) – less than the majority of contemporary super sport 600s!

The R1 project began in 1995, when Yamaha engineer Kunihito Miwa set about designing and building the fastest, lightest, and best-handling sports bike possible. The result was considerably smaller and lighter than its predecessor, the YZF 1000R (Thunderace).

A COMPACT ENGINE

The R1 featured a compact version of Yamaha's familiar 20-valve, four-cylinder, across-the-frame engine. Displacing 998cc (74.0x58.0mm bore and stroke), it employed a one-piece cylinder and crankcase assembly. A sophisticated exhaust ultimate power valve (EXUP) system took into account engine

speed, throttle position, and even the rate at which the throttle was opened. It also provided additional mid-range torque.

The R1's engine sat well forward in the aluminium, twin-beam, Deltabox frame, allowing a longer rear swinging arm (also aluminium) to improve stability.

MULTI-ADJUSTABLE SUSPENSION

The suspension was multi-adjustable, the inverted front fork featuring extra rebound at the end of its travel to help keep the front wheel down under hard acceleration. Miwa and his engineers also paid particular attention to the brakes and wheels (150mm/6in wide at the rear with a 190-section tyre).

Although largely conceived as a roadster, in many ways, the R1 had been designed like a race bike, particularly in respect of its "minimum weight" theme. For example, the four-piston, front brake calipers had been lightened to reduce

facing page Just as Suzuki's
GSX-R changed 750cc sports-
bike design in 1985, so did
Yamaha's 1,000cc R1 when it
appeared in late 1997, with its
ultra-lightweight chassis and
awesome performance.

left Designer Kunihito Miwa and
his team gave the R1 some nice
touches, including these footrest
controls...

below ...and streamlined,
car-type headlamps.

unsprung weight, while the three-spoke alloy wheels were
hollow. Cutting weight, Miwa reasoned, helped improve
suspension performance.

ENGINE TRACTABILITY

Another aspect of the engine (common to all big-bore, five-
valves-per-cylinder Yamaha engines) was its tractability. In
standard, untuned form, the bike could be ridden smoothly at
32km/h (20mph) in top gear and, with little or no hesitation,
accelerated all the way to the 11,500rpm red line.

Miwa updated the R1 for 2000, notably with a new fairing
to improve aerodynamic efficiency and reduce rider fatigue.
There was also a new titanium silencer.

Suzuki's answer to the R1 was the GSX-R1000; Kawasaki
introduced the ZX-10. This led to an ongoing battle between
the three manufacturers in the showroom and on the track.

1998 YAMAHA R1 SPECIFICATIONS

Engine Liquid-cooled, double-overhead-
camshaft, 20-valve, across-the-frame,
four-cylinder

Displacement 998cc

Bore and stroke 74.0x58.0mm

Ignition Electronic

Gearbox Six-speed, foot-change

Final drive Chain

Frame Aluminium, twin-beam, Deltabox

Dry weight 177kg (390lb)

Maximum power 160bhp at 11,500rpm

Top speed 282km/h (175mph)

MV AGUSTA F4

Hailed by many as the ultimate modern motorcycle, the MV Agusta F4 could easily have been a Cagiva or Ducati – or even a Ferrari. The fact that it was an MV is a fitting tribute to one of the strangest of all bike projects.

BIRTH OF AN IDEA

The original concept for the machine came from conversations between Claudio Castiglioni, Cagiva's boss, and his chief designer, Massimo Tamburini. Piero Ferrari, son of Enzo Ferrari, also contributed.

The first rumours concerning a brand-new, Cagiva-inspired sports bike began to circulate at the beginning of the 1990s. Then, at the launch of the Ferrari 465 GT car, a photograph of the new motorcycle engine was shown by mistake. As a result, Castiglioni was forced to confirm that it was being developed in conjunction with Ferrari, and that he and Piero Ferrari had actually tested the prototype machine.

DEVELOPMENT GLITCHES

Cagiva suffered financial problems during the mid-1990s, which slowed development at the company's secret hilltop research centre in San Marino, but in the spring of 1998, the first example of the long-awaited machine appeared. From the start, it was badged as an MV Agusta. (Cagiva had purchased the famous marque's name some years earlier, and, having sold Ducati to the American Texas Pacific Group, it could not have used that name.)

The F4's styling was superior to that of every other series-production sports bike in the world, while it bristled with innovative technical features.

TECHNICAL DETAILS

The 749.8cc (73.8x43.8mm bore and stroke), liquid-cooled, four-valves-per-cylinder, double-overhead-camshaft, across-the-frame, four-cylinder engine was equipped with a radical, radial-valve cylinder head, and the very latest Weber-Marelli electronic fuel injection and ignition systems. It was combined with a removable (cassette-type), six-speed gearbox.

The F4's frame was a combination of steel and aluminium components, while its steering-head angle was fully adjustable. At the front was a specially built, inverted Showa fork assembly with an Öhlins hydraulic steering damper mounted across the frame. The exhaust outlets were beneath the seat, this being a Tamburini styling trademark.

Tamburini also conceived a particularly innovative front light arrangement. The twin stacked polyellipsoidal units gave the F4 a unique appearance, while allowing a very narrow fairing for maximum aerodynamic advantage.

A naked version, stripped of its bodywork, the Brutale, was introduced in 2002. By 2005 there was a larger-engined F4 1000 sportster, plus the distinctively customized America with its eye-catching red, blue, and white paint job.

2000 MV AGUSTA F4 750
SPECIFICATIONS

Engine Liquid-cooled, double-overhead-camshaft, 16-valve, across-the-frame, four-cylinder

Displacement 749cc

Bore and stroke 73.8x43.8mm

Ignition Electronic, integrated with fuel injection

Gearbox Six-speed, foot-change, cassette type

Final drive Chain

Frame Steel and aluminium, fully-adjustable steering head

Dry weight 180kg (397lb)

Maximum power 137bhp at 12,600rpm

Top speed 282km/h (175mph)

GLOSSARY

Aerodynamics A science that focuses on the movement of solid forms through the air.

Air cooling A method of removing heat from engine cylinder barrels and heads by the natural flow of air over them. The components are finned to aid the process.

AIV Automatic inlet valve. Activated by engine suction; forerunner of the mechanically operated valve.

Belt drive A leather or fabric belt running from the engine or gearbox to the rear wheel.

Bhp Brake horsepower. A measure of an engine's power output.

Bore and stroke ratio The ratio of an engine's cylinder diameter to its piston stroke.

Boxer An engine with horizontal cylinders.

Caliper A clamping device containing hydraulically operated pistons; part of a disc brake.

Cam A device for opening and closing a valve.

Camshaft The mounting shaft for a cam; can be in low, high or overhead position.

Carburettor Produces the air/fuel mixture for the engine.

Chain drive Primary form of drive from engine to gearbox, and secondary (final) from gearbox to rear wheel.

Combustion chamber Area where the fuel/air mixture is compressed and ignited, between the piston and cylinder head.

Connecting rod Assembly that joins the piston to the crankshaft; also con-rod.

Compression ratio The amount by which the fuel/air mixture is compressed by the piston in the combustion chamber.

Crankcase The casing enclosing the crankshaft (and gearbox in a unit-construction engine).

Crankshaft The shaft that converts the vertical motion of the piston into a rotary movement.

Cylinder Contains the piston and is capped by the cylinder head. Upper portion forms the combustion chamber where the fuel/air mixture is compressed and burned to provide power.

Cylinder head Caps the top of the cylinder. In a four-stroke engine, it usually houses the valves and, in some cases, one or two camshafts.

Damper Fitted to slow movement in the suspension system, or act as a crankshaft balance (*see also* shock absorber).

Disc valve An induction system found on some two-stroke engines; usually a series of discs, located in the crankcase, rather than the cylinder barrel.

Displacement The engine capacity or volume displaced by the movement of the piston from its bottom-dead-centre position to top dead centre.

Deltabox A box-section, aluminium frame.

DOHC Double overhead camshaft. Two camshafts mounted in the cylinder head.

Dry sump An engine lubrication system, in which oil is contained in a separate reservoir, and carried to and from the engine by a pair of pumps.

Duplex frame A frame with twin main tubes to support the engine, rather than a single tube.

Earles fork A front fork design incorporating long leading links connected by a rigid pivot behind the front wheel.

Face cam A similar arrangement to an overhead camshaft, but without the cost and complexity.

Featherbed A Norton frame, designed by Rex McCandless.

Flat-twin An engine with two horizontally opposed cylinders.

Flywheel Fitted to the crankshaft, this heavy wheel smoothes intermittent firing pulses and helps smooth running.

Friction drive An early form of drive, using discs that press against each other instead of chains and gears.

Gearbox A case containing trains of gear wheels that can be moved to provide different ratios.

Gear ratio The ratio between the input and output speeds of a train of gears; indicates the difference between engine revolutions and rear wheel revolutions.

High camshaft A camshaft mounted high in the engine to shorten the pushrods in an overhead-valve design.

Hp Horsepower. A method of indicating engine displacement, used on early British machines; not to be confused with bhp.

Intercooling A system for cooling the fuel/air mixture as it passes from a turbocharger or supercharger to the cylinder, increasing power output.

IOE Inlet over exhaust. A common arrangement in early motorcycles: overhead inlet valve and side exhaust valve.

Leaf spring Several metal blades clamped together; used in early motorcycle suspension systems.

Liquid cooling A method of removing heat from engine cylinder barrels and heads by allowing water to flow through passages formed in them. Flow may be achieved by siphon or pump, the water passing through a radiator to cool it.

Magneto A high-tension dynamo that produces current for the ignition spark; superseded by coil ignition.

Main bearing A bearing in which the crankshaft runs.

Manifold A collection of pipes for supplying the fuel/air mixture to the engine, or for removing exhaust gases.

Monocoque Bodywork that doubles as a supporting structure for a machine's mechanical components.

OHC Overhead camshaft. A single camshaft mounted in the cylinder head.

OHV Overhead valve. An inlet or exhaust valve mounted in the cylinder head.

Piston Moves up and down the cylinder, drawing in the fuel/air mixture and compressing it, before being driven down by combustion to turn the crankshaft, then forcing out the exhaust gases; also used in hydraulic brake calipers.

Piston-port induction A method of supplying the fuel/air mixture to a two-stroke engine via the cylinder barrel.

Pushrod Operates an overhead valve by riding on a cam below the cylinder.

Reed valve Improves induction in a two-stroke engine via the cylinder; installed between cylinder and carburettor.

Shaft drive A final drive system, using a rigid shaft that runs between the engine and rear wheel.

Shock absorber Fitted to slow movement in the suspension system, or act as a crankshaft balance (*see also* damper).

SV Side valve. An inlet or exhaust valve mounted in the cylinder barrel.

Silencer Fitted to the exhaust system of an engine to reduce the pressure of the exhaust gases and lessen noise.

Swinging arm A form of rear suspension, in which an arm carries the wheel and is attached to the frame at its forward end by a pivot.

Torque Twisting force in a shaft; can be measured to determine at what speed an engine develops maximum pulling power.

Wet sump An engine lubrication system, in which the oil is contained within a sump that forms part of the crankcase.

INDEX

Every so often a unique snapshot of times gone by is discovered in a dusty vault or in shoeboxes in an attic by an enthusiastic amateur photographer. They are living history. Each and every one of us cannot resist the temptation as we marvel at the quality of the images, to let our mind drift back to the good old days and wonder what it was really like.

We at Mortons Motorcycle Media, market-leading publishers of classic and vintage titles, own one of the largest photographic archives of its kind in the world. It is a treasure trove of millions of motorcycle and related images, many of which have never seen the light of day since they were filed away in the dark-room almost 100 years ago.

Perhaps the biggest gem of all is our collection of glass plates – almost two tons of them to be precise! They represent a largely hitherto unseen look into our motorcycling heritage from the turn of the century. Many of the plates are priceless and capture an era long gone when the pace of life was much slower and traffic jams were unheard of. We are delighted to be associated with well-known author Mick Walker in the production of this book and hope you enjoy the images from our archive.

Terry Clark,
Managing Director,
Mortons Media Group Ltd

"I am privileged to have access to the Mortons Motorcycle Media Archive, which I consider to be the finest in the world and a national treasure."
MICK WALKER

ACKNOWLEDGMENTS

The author would like to thank the following for their assistance:

Colin Seeley, for kindly agreeing to pen the Foreword
Alan Wilson of Redline Books
Gary Houlden of Webbs Yamaha Centre, Peterborough
Terry Rudd of TRM, Holbeach
Keith Davies of Three Cross Motorcycles
Jane Scayman of Mortons Media Group
Livio Lodi of the Ducati Museum, Bologna
The National Motorcycle Museum, Birmingham
Pooks Motor Bookshop, Leicester
Steve Bedford
Andrew Hunt
Philip Tooth
Martin Philp
Vic Bates
Doreen and John Hynes
Patty Ruston

PICTURE CREDITS